THE
GODS
OF GREECE

THE GODS
OF GREECE

Arianna Stassinopoulos and Roloff Beny

HARRY N. ABRAMS INC. PUBLISHERS
NEW YORK

To our fathers
Constantine Stassinopoulos and Charles J. F. Beny

PAGE I Fragment of a marble gravestone showing the
head of a discus thrower, *c.* 560 BC.

FRONTISPIECE Detail of an Archaic gravestone from
Laurion in Attica, *c.* 500 BC.

'Is he from our world? No, his deep nature
grows out of both of the kingdoms.
He can bend down the branches of the willow best
Who has experienced the roots of the willow.'
RAINER MARIA RILKE

Library of Congress Cataloging in Publication Data

Stassinopoulos, Arianna.
The gods of Greece.

1. Gods, Greek. 2. Mythology, Greek.
I. Beny, Roloff. II. Title.
BL782.S8 1983   292'.211   82–13920
ISBN 0–8109–0958–8

Printed and bound in Italy

CONTENTS

INTRODUCTION · 7

THE GODS

42 · POSEIDON   HERA · 161

53 · APOLLO   HESTIA · 168

69 · ARTEMIS   ARES · 170

78 · APHRODITE   HEPHAISTOS · 175

97 · DIONYSOS   DEMETER · 178

115 · ZEUS   HADES · 187

138 · ATHENA   HERMES · 190

EPILOGUE · 203

MAP OF ANCIENT GREECE · 208

AUTHORS' ACKNOWLEDGEMENTS · 209

NOTES 210

LIST OF ILLUSTRATIONS · 213

INDEX · 215

INTRODUCTION
Ancient Gods in Modern Faces

EVER SINCE I CAN REMEMBER I have lived under the spell of the Greek gods. Their stories were part of my life before I could read, their names were part of my vocabulary before I could spell and their personalities were alive in my imagination long before I had started drawing distinctions between imagination and reality.

I loved them long before I could understand them, and it is this love and wonder – childlike and timeless at the same time – that I have tried to capture in this book. I want it to be a celebration of the gods, not a scientific dissection of their corpses. Only by celebrating the gods and being moved by them will we be able to rescue them from the hands of philologists and mythologists busy burying them under piles of scientific data. Nor is this an idle rescue operation. At a time when myth has become practically a synonym for falsehood and dry rationality reigns supreme, the Greek gods can guide us to forgotten dimensions of our lives and of ourselves.

The Greek mythological culture began to form in the dim and distant late Bronze Age around the shores of Crete and the grim citadels of the Argolid. Since that time it has hung over the whole of the 'Western adventure', right up to the Oedipus complex, the Apollo spacecrafts and the Saturn and Poseidon missiles of our own day.

The gods may have gone underground for centuries at a time but, like an underground river flowing through Western culture, they have continued to send up springs and fountains inspiring, shaping and fertilizing the Western imagination, even when it was suffocating in the dross of exclusive materialism.

And we can still respond to the gods and goddesses, nymphs and heroes, of ancient Greece at some profound, obscure level of our imagination because they correspond to realities within ourselves and point to realities beyond

Gold funerary mask from Mycenae, 16th century BC. 'The fear of death is indeed the pretence of wisdom, and not real wisdom, for it is a pretence of knowing the unknown; and no one knows whether death, which men in their fear apprehend to be the greatest evil, may not be the greatest good. . . .'
PLATO, *Apology of Socrates*

themselves long before we have interpreted and understood them. When we look at the gods through the prism of the age of reason we miss their symbolic significance for our lives. We still have the magnificence of the stories, but we lose the living truth they spring from. But once we discover the connecting thread between the old myths and ourselves, we become open to dimensions in the stories of the gods which reveal new depths in them and new vital meaning.

The whole of Greek mythology comes alive when we see the Greek gods and goddesses not as beings external to ourselves but as parts of our own inner pantheon. When we recognize the psychological forces personified in the gods, we see them for what they are: not self-conscious poetic fancies, but universal images that compel us to attune to the 'mythic' unity – the pattern and wholeness underlying the fragmentary moments, decisions and events of everyday life.

Then the myths 'are no longer stories in an illustrated book. *We* are those stories, and we illustrate them with our lives.' The myths of the gods, through the conflicts and resolutions they portray, move our own conflicts and problems into a deeper background away from the trivial and mundane. It is through our conflicts, dilemmas and anxieties, as well as through our joys and accomplishments, that the gods enter our lives and become real, giving to our experiences an added dimension of depth and significance. Being a wife, bearing a daughter, experiencing jealousy, aggression or sexual passion – these are all everyday mysteries that we take for granted but which the myths of Hera or Demeter, Aphrodite or Ares, help us enter more deeply and understand more fully, more consciously and more symbolically. 'To the imagination the sacred is self-evident. To believe in Aphrodite and Ares merely means that one believes that the poetic myths about them do justice to the forces of sex and aggression as human beings experience them in nature and their own lives.'

'Everything is full of Gods' THALES

'Everything is full of Gods', wrote Thales. 'Zeus is the air, Zeus the earth, and Zeus the sky, Zeus everything, and all that is more than these', proclaimed Aeschylus. 'Soul is mingled in the whole', explained Aristotle.

No part of life was complete for the Greeks without the divine, and nothing was more natural than to be surrounded by gods and filled with them. Personification was the most distinctive mode of Greek thinking. Psychic powers, once personified, affected men's hearts and not just their minds. They were 'real demons to be worshipped and propitiated and no mere fragments of the imagination. And, as is well known, they were actually worshipped in every Greek city. To mention Athens alone, we find altars and sanctuaries of Victory, Fortune, Friendship, Forgetfulness, Modesty, Mercy, Peace, and many more....' The gods are so actively and naturally present in everyday life that holiness has no place in Greek religion. Miracles have no place in it either, or to put it another way, everything is a miracle.

The gods roamed the earth, clad in mist, in hundreds of guises, guardians of mortal men, meting out justice, giving wealth and happiness and taking them away. Nothing important happens without the gods manifesting themselves, yet the natural course never seems interrupted. We hear, indeed we see in our mind's eye, how a god whispers a saving device to a warrior, we hear that he stirs spirit and kindles courage, that he makes limbs nimble and gives a faltering arm strength. But these divine interventions, far from being miraculous, are seen as the very essence of everyday experience because the divine is seen as the basis of all being and reality.

The sanctifying of the everyday, one of the highest ideals of all religions, is here a living truth. 'The faculty which in other religions is constantly being thwarted and inhibited here flowers forth with the admirable assurance of genius – the faculty of seeing the world in the light of the divine, not a world yearned for, aspired to, or mystically present in rare ecstatic experiences, but the world into which we were born, part of which we are, interwoven with it through our senses and, through our minds, drawing from it for all its abundance and vitality.'

The Atlas metope from the temple of Zeus at Olympia depicts a scene which compellingly captures the ever-present guardian quality of the gods. Herakles has taken over from Atlas the support of the world; the arch of heaven rests heavily on his shoulders; it threatens to crush him. Unnoticed, the bright and noble figure of Athena has stepped out behind him and, with the indescribable dignity of posture which is the hallmark of Greek divinity, she gently touches the burden. And Herakles, who cannot see her, feels that his strength has miraculously expanded and he is now able to perform what seemed impossible.

At the moment of severest trial, Athena always appears at the side of the mighty heroes she protects. 'Of all mankind', she tells Odysseus in the *Odyssey*, 'thou are easily foremost, both in counsel and speech, and among all gods I win fame for my wisdom and cleverness.' This is what distinguishes and binds them together. She stands by Odysseus' side through all his trials as the divine embodiment of the wisdom, shrewdness and grandeur that are already present in Odysseus himself.

This kind of 'coincidence' – the sudden appearance of the gods, the '*deus ex machina*' which is at the centre of Greek myth and Greek tragedy – stops appearing improbable and infantile when we translate the nearness of the divine at the moments of greatest trial into our everyday language: such and such misfortune or hardship, we say, 'brought out the best in him', or 'put him in touch with resources he never knew he had' or 'he became a different person'. When we approach the gods in this spirit, they awaken in us a trust in our own hidden powers, our own connection with the divine, our own capacity to create miracles and experience transformation.

'We make our destinies by our choice of Gods' VIRGIL

What Virgil's poetic genius knew instinctively, modern psychology confirms empirically. The structure of our being is a field where rival forces – many of them unconscious – contend for power. Our theology may have replaced the gods of the ancient world by one god, omniscient and omnipotent, but psychologically we are still pagans. The state of wholeness and integration, implied by psychological monotheism, remains for most an aspiration rather than reality. When our true self is enthroned at the centre of our being over and above the many selves, the many powers engaged in an inner struggle, then we will indeed have reached the kingdom of one god. But, in the meantime, our being is more accurately described as a kingdom in civil war. And to call the contending powers in us 'gods', as the ancient world did, is to acknowledge both their emotional power over us and the need to propitiate them, to attend to them, to give them conscious recognition – because if we do not, they rise and take their revenge. The neutral language of complexes, archetypes, super-egos and sub-personalities which has dominated our century since Freud popularized the unconscious may sound modern and scientific, but it lacks the emotional immediacy that these forces evoke – and can still evoke – in man when they are personified as gods and goddesses.

'If the unconscious figures', wrote Jung, 'are not accorded the dignity of spontaneously effective factors, one becomes the victim of a one-sided belief in the conscious, which finally leads to a state of mental tension. Catastrophes are then bound to occur, because, despite all one's consciousness, the dark psychic powers have been overlooked. It is not we who personify them; they have a personal nature from the very beginning.' Acknowledging the personal, distinct nature of these forces slumbering in our unconscious can help us end the delusion of unity and accept the multiplicity of the primordial powers affecting our lives. We have all the gods and goddesses in us, but in differing degrees of intensity – some stronger, some weaker, some in the foreground, some in the background – with a particular god dominating our lives at a particular stage only to retreat when we move on to a different stage.

The conflicts in our lives and our relationships are conflicts among the

Archaic goddess of fertility suckling twins, 540–530 BC. 'Divine Earth, mother of men and of the blessed gods, you nourish all, you give all, you bring all to fruition, and you destroy all.'
Orphic Hymn to Mother Earth

gods. In Virgil's story of Dido and Aeneas the protagonists are under the sway of two different goddesses – Dido is ruled by Juno (Hera), the goddess of marriage and permanent unions, Aeneas by Venus (Aphrodite), the goddess of passionate love that refuses to be tied down. They worship at different altars, they embody different ways of loving, and because they fail to see the other's god, the end is tragedy. 'I saw the god', says Aeneas as he is about to leave Dido behind in Carthage. 'I saw the god, as clear as day, with my own eyes, and these ears drank in the words he uttered. No more reproaches then – they only torture us both. God's will, not mine, says "Italy".' Aeneas chose the god to follow and the choice sealed his destiny. Dido's choice sealed hers.

Antagonism among the different gods runs through the whole of Greek mythology, and the classic conflict that has dominated Western literature and has even entered our everyday language is the conflict between Apollo and Dionysos – between the Apollonian and the Dionysian powers in man, between the need for order, balance and clarity and the instinct for freedom, ecstasy and exaltation. In different men, or at different stages in the life of the same man, one god or the other holds sway. The vivid lesson of the Greek myths and of Greek tragedy is that unless both gods are given their due, there is a high price to pay. The need for their reconciliation was even institutionalized in Delphi. Delphi was Apollo's home but, during the winter months, he ceded his shrine to Dionysos, and the Dionysian festival was carried out in its full glory by an officially sanctioned band of Maenads.

'Thou that leadest the dance of the fiery stars,' cried Sophocles through his chorus in *Antigone*, 'watcher over the nocturnal sky, Zeus-born child, appear, lord, with thine attendant Thyiades, who all night long in frenzied ecstasy dance thy dance. . . .' The need for Dionysian ecstasy was given its sanctioned place in Apollonian order so that it would not rise out of its neglected depths and overthrow it.

We bring about the fights of the gods when we refuse to recognize the separate claims of the forces they represent, when we reject one in favour of the other. Then the rejected god goes underground and only surfaces to wreak his vengeance as he does in Euripides' *Bacchae* where the grim feast Dionysos demands culminates in a mother's ritual killing of her son under the god's manic influence. Or as he does in Aeschylus' *Bassarids*, where Orpheus neglects his worship for that of the sun and ends by being torn to pieces by the rejected god's followers. It is madness, the poets tell us, to choke off and deny the elemental forces in us. And madness leads to madness. We can choose the god we owe our primary allegiance to, but only if we remember to pay our dues to the rest of our inner pantheon.

'God moves as the beloved moves the lover' ARISTOTLE

'First of all, Chaos came into being, next broad-bosomed Earth, the solid and eternal home of all, and Eros the most beautiful of the immortal gods, who in every man and every god softens the sinews and overpowers the prudent purpose of the mind.'

In Hesiod's *Theogony*, Eros is the first god born out of Chaos at the beginning of creation. He is the creative energy ever present in all things, constantly driving them to relationship and proliferation. He is the connecting principle, the god who embodies the spirit of relatedness. Eros predates the Olympian gods, which is only right since without connection and relationship there can be no life – only divisions and lifeless separateness. In late Greek myths, Eros becomes the son of Aphrodite and Ares, the goddess of love and the god of war. But what this myth gains in picturesque detail, it loses in power, until by Roman times the oldest of the gods, the god whose realm extends from the 'endless space of heavens to the dark abyss of hell', is reduced to little, mischievous Cupid, piercing the hearts of lovers.

Eros is the force, the god, that breeds in us the longing that drives us to physical love and beyond it, ever onward, to the love that yearns for the unattainable, the incomprehensible. So Eros is the god presiding over both man's primordial nature and the highest form of man's spiritual longings. He cannot be grasped because he grasps *us*. He cannot be understood but only experienced as he shoots through every aspect of our lives. According to Plato, the impulse to seek what is higher – 'the beyond' – comes first from falling in love with visible, physical beauty. Then this impulse, a kind of divine madness, lifts the soul up and guides it to enter the path which leads to the truth. In the *Symposium*, the highest form of birth engendered by Eros is self-birth in the 'rebirth of the initiate as a divine being'.

The passionate desire to love and possess another physically, the passionate desire to know, the passionate desire to be reborn as a divine being, are all different manifestations of Eros at work. The oldest god is the life-force behind all movement in the universe.

'That which is above is as that which is below' HERMETICA

'Hesiod and Homer', wrote Herodotus, 'are the ones who provided the Greeks with a theogony, gave the gods their names, distinguished their attributes and functions, and defined the various types.' But it was Homer who bequeathed to the classical Greeks the brilliant, clear-cut, fully-formed figures of the twelve Olympians who still today embody for us the Hellenic spirit. Single altars were erected to them, the Greeks swore by them as a unity ('By the Twelve!'), and when Alexander reached India, he built an altar to the twelve to mark the eastern-most point of his conquests.

Homer's religion was a daylight religion of joy, strength and beauty, it was the background to the official city-state religions, it was part of the mental equipment with which every Greek grew up, but it was not all. Greek religion, like every religion that is alive and evolving rather than a frozen system of thought, was full of paradox. For a start, the twelve gods were really fourteen: Zeus, Hera, Poseidon, Apollo, Artemis, Ares, Aphrodite, Hermes, Athena, Demeter, Hephaistos, Hestia, Dionysos and Hades. To keep the number to twelve, Hestia, the goddess of the hearth, was often left at home so that a place could be made for Dionysos, a later admission to the circle of the Olympians. And Hades, the brother of Zeus and Poseidon, was permanently consigned to the Underworld. They played no smaller part in people's lives, though, nor were they any less worshipped by them.

Side by side with the Olympians there were the chthonic (subterranean) deities, local spirits or demons whose cults went back far earlier than the Homeric poems and whose worship remained alive in people's hearts. The Greeks could not see a river without seeing a river god, a tree without seeing a tree spirit, a spring without seeing the Naiad who made her home there. So to experience the Greek religion in all its dimensions – and understand ourselves in all our dimensions – a descent to the chthonic depths is as important as a flight to Olympos.

And when we descend to the depths we encounter, first and foremost, Gaia, the Mother Goddess: 'One race there is of men and one of gods, but from one mother, Earth, draw we both our breath.' The principal Olympian goddesses – Athena, Artemis, Hera and Aphrodite – were each identified with one aspect of the feminine, but the Mother Goddess was, and remains, the feminine in all its primordial power, the instinctive source of renewal with which life has to remain connected, for otherwise it withers away.

Homer's vision of the Underworld paralleled his vision of death as the beginning of an existence deprived of all that made life worth living. The miserable Homeric shades wandered in Hades bodiless, bloodless and boneless, seeking energy and animation from the living through the blood vapours of sacrificed animals. In the *Odyssey*, Achilles in the Underworld cries out that he would rather be a labourer working for a poor man on earth than rule as a king among the dead.

At the same time, Homer bestowed on the Greeks another vision of life after death in the earthly paradise of the Elysian Fields, reserved for men who had been absorbed into the family of the gods. In the *Odyssey*, he gives us an example of this blissful immortality in the promise made to Menelaus:

But as for thee, Menelaus . . . to the Elysian plain and the farthest borders of the earth shall the immortals send thee . . . where life is easier for men. No snow is there, nor heavy storm, nor rain ever, but always Okeanos sends forth the breezes of clear-breathing Zephyr to bring refreshment to men. Thither shall they send thee because thou hast Helen to wife and art in their eyes son-in-law of Zeus.

By the fifth century BC, through the spread of the Eleusinian Mysteries connected with Demeter and the descent of her daughter Persephone into the Underworld, the gulf between mortal men and the immortal gods was bridged not by adoption into the family of the Homeric gods but by initiation into the rites of the Underworld and the mysteries of their own highest nature. 'Happy is he', writes Pindar, 'who having seen these rites goes below the hollow earth: for he knows the end of life and he knows its god-sent beginnings.' And Sophocles calls those mortals who depart for Hades having seen these rites thrice happy: 'For to them alone it is granted to have found life there.'

The life they find there is not the flesh-and-blood life of Homer's earthly paradise but the life of the divine soul. Across the daylight world of the Homeric gods, the Eleusinian Mysteries linked up with the chthonic cults which Homer never entirely supplanted. They emphasized the kinship of man with all the other creatures of the earth and the kinship – indeed the ultimate identity – between human and divine nature. The mythological brotherhood of Zeus and Hades becomes a psychological reality. One sees the world 'from above and through the light, the other from below and into its darkness'. To live fully the two perspectives must co-exist. Hades' other name was Pluto which in Greek means riches, wealth – the riches of the invisible, of discovering the depths of the soul not only 'after life' but within life. The move into the Underworld, as the journey into the unconscious has shown in our century, is not a move forward in time but a move downward and inward, concurrent with our daily life and enriching our daily concerns with the dimension of soul and depth.

Hades is the unseen yet absolutely present god, and even his propitiation is inward and invisible. 'Death is the only god', writes Aeschylus, 'who loves not gifts and cares not for sacrifices or libation, who has no altar and receives no hymns. . . .' His main connection with men, apart from their direct descent into the underworld of the soul, is through dreams. In the *Odyssey*, Homer places dreams in the 'House of Hades' or in their own realm in the 'Western Ocean' where the sun sets and night begins. And the god who bridges the two realms, the god to whom men turn for dreams is Hermes – the Olympian who, above all others, embodies the principle of connection. He connects gods to each other, men to the gods, and the chthonic, the earthly, element in men and gods to the divine. As the god who guides men in both their descent to the Underworld and their flight to Olympos, he is the god in whom all contradictions between the brilliance of Homer's daylight world and the darkness and depth of the mystery cults are reconciled in a living, pulsating, reality.

'I beget the light, but the darkness also is of my nature'　HERMETICA

> Night gave birth to hateful Destruction and the black Spectre and Death; she also bore Sleep and the race of Dreams – all these the dark goddess Night bore without sleeping with any male. Next she gave birth to Blame and painful Grief, and also the Fates and the pitiless Spectres of Vengeance: it is these goddesses who keep account of the transgressions of men and of gods, and they never let their terrible anger end till they have brought punishment down on the head of the transgressor. Deadly Night also bore Retribution to plague men, then Deceit and Love and accursed Old Age and stubborn Strife. Hateful Strife gave birth to painful Distress and Distraction and Famine and tearful Sorrow; also Wars and Battles and Murders and Slaughters; also Feuds and Lying Words and Angry Words; also Lawlessness and Madness – two sisters that go together. . . .

And so Hesiod goes on in his *Theogony*, immediately evoking the truth that there is darkness as well as light in the universe, terror as well as beauty. In Homer, the darkness and the light are not separate divinities but contained within each god. The gods who create are the gods who destroy. In dramatic contrast to the idea that has dominated Western culture of one great god and one great, contending principle of evil, each Greek god contains a polarity, an inner tension, a light and a dark side that casts a shadow variously shaped according to his particular character: sometimes vengeful, sometimes cheating, sometimes quarrelsome or belligerent. So man is as much in the image of the gods and goddesses when he is creative, joyful, triumphant, as when his dark underside is showing.

The Greek gods are so human, we say, as we conjure up Hera's jealousy and Artemis' vengeance, Zeus' lust and Demeter's grief. 'The gods are our brothers', wrote Pindar. But it would be truer to say that they are, in fact, ourselves. The tensions and ambiguities of each god puzzled and disturbed me for a long time, not because I cannot accept paradox, but because I could not see the ultimate reconciliation. Now I see that the reconciliation is not within each god but among all the gods and all the gods' aspects within man. 'The antithetical powers collide eternally; they meet, fight, conquer and are conquered, become reconciled for a brief moment, and then begin to battle again throughout the Universe – from the invisible whirlpool in a drop of water to the endless cataclysm of stars in the Galaxy.'

There is no firm line in Greek mythology between virtue and sin, heroes

RIGHT Terracotta statue of youth found at Lavinium in Italy, 4th–3rd centuries BC.

PAGE 18 'Mourning Athena', *c*.450 BC.
'The wounder and healer, the destroyer and creator; the Goddess who delights in the turmoil of arms and in stormy, pitched battle yet instructs man in the arts of weaving and of pressing oil from the olive.'
　　　KARL PHILIPP MORITZ

PAGE 19 Winged Nike, the goddess of victory, *c*.410 BC.
'The giver of sweet gifts who on gold-gleaming Olympos at Zeus' side determines for gods and men success in noble endeavours.'　　BACCHYLIDES

PAGE 20 Marble *kore*, holding an offering to Athena, *c*.520 BC.

PAGE 21 The Calf-bearer, *c*.570 BC, carrying on his shoulders his sacrifice to Athena.

and villains, perfect gods and imperfect men. The psychic forces the gods represent, negative and positive, are not isolated in neat compartments; there is a constant flow and connection among them. Even love and hate blend – after all, Ares and Aphrodite were secret lovers. What Kazantzakis called 'the ascent toward composition, toward life, toward immortality' and 'the descent toward decomposition, toward matter, toward death' are two streams that in the Greek myths merge in a living reality with no sense of paradox or contradiction. 'What is our duty?... Out of things and flesh, out of hunger, out of fear, out of virtue and sin, struggle continually to create God.' In our sickness and suffering, our failures and limitations, we are still living out another aspect of the gods. In our isolation, our fear of intimacy and commitment, we can turn to Artemis as our patron goddess; in our impulse to enchant and to trap we embody the destructive side of Aphrodite; in our over-identification with the rational side of ourselves we are living out the dark side of Apollo's brilliance.

During the Corybantic rituals, the patient found, by way of music, which god was causing his trouble: that was the diagnosis and the beginning of healing. What was a symptom, a fear, an obsession, became a god that had to be given his due. We are created in the gods' images and, therefore, can do nothing and feel nothing that has not already found expression in their behaviour. 'It is not a matter of indifference', wrote Jung, 'whether one calls something a "mania" or a "god". To serve a mania is detestable and undignified, but to serve a god is full of meaning.' By seeing our personal fears and inadequacies in a mythical light we are more likely to stop evading them – and by accepting them, we can begin to transform them.

Perhaps the greatest expression of such a transformation was given by Aeschylus in the *Eumenides*. Orestes is being pursued by the Erinyes, the dreaded Furies, the daughters of the Night. They demand revenge. Then Athena, representing the new, free, Olympian spirit, effects a reconciliation between the light of the new order and the darkness of the elemental deities, not by defeating and suppressing them but by offering them a place within the divine order, by promising them an altar and high honours instead of curses from the people. The transformation of the darkness takes place by acknowledging it and integrating it with the light. 'This thing of darkness, I acknowledge mine', says Prospero of Caliban in *The Tempest*. And where Shakespeare followed, Aeschylus and Athena had led the way.

'Not even a God can cope with Necessity'   PLATO

'Zeus' second consort was Themis (Law), and that radiant lady gave birth to the Hours – Good Order, Justice, and prosperous Peace – who hourly attend the labours of mankind, and to the Fates – Clotho (Spinner), Lachesis

PAGE 22 Lapith woman from the west pediment of the temple of Zeus at Olympia, *c.*460 BC, depicting the battle between the Lapiths and the Centaurs.

PAGE 23 Apollo presiding over the battle between the Centaurs and the Lapiths, from the same pediment.

LEFT Marble statue of Asklepios, the son of Apollo and the god of healing and medicine, 2nd century BC.

(Allotter), and Atropus (Inflexible) – to whom Zeus gave the great privilege of distributing good and evil among mankind.'

The image of the Fates permeates Greek mythology and poetry from Hesiod onward. Plato describes in detail the way the three Fates portion out each soul's destiny 'resolved on from untold ages'. From Lachesis the soul goes on to Clotho to ratify the lot it received, and from her to Atropus 'to make the web of its destiny irreversible, and then without a backward look it passeth beneath the throne of Necessity'. The staff and hook of the spindle of Necessity, through which all the orbits turn, were made of adamant, and the three Fates were pictured, each on her throne, clad in white, singing in unison: 'Lachesis singing the things that were, Clotho the things that are, and Atropus the things that are to be.'

'As for death, it will come whenever the Fates with their spindle decree', laments the seventh-century poet Callinos. And not even the gods, Homer tells us, can save a man however much they love him. In the *Iliad*, Zeus himself cries out over the fate of his son Sarpedon who, the Fates have decreed, must die by the hand of Patroclus.

Necessity is 'that which cannot not be', and the gods who could break all the laws of space, time, gravity, causality – and indeed morality – had to obey the laws of Necessity. However irrational and incredible their behaviour, it was not arbitrary. Necessity rules – even on Olympos.

'And indeed, as far as godhead was concerned, even Zeus could think, reason, learn, and improve morally through time' JOSEPH CAMPBELL

'If the gods do aught ugly, they are not gods!' cries one of Euripides' characters. In one sentence he sums up our modern ambivalence toward the ancient gods. We want our gods moral, just, pure – perfect. We want good gods. Instead we are confronted with gods who cheat, lie, kill and destroy, and our response is to dismiss them as ornaments, poetic fancies. To approach the gods through moral judgement and our fixed categories of good and evil is, as Blake puts it, to negate the imagination and ignore the passions, irrationalities and destructive urges which dominate so many of our fantasies and pathologies and which, indeed, have shaped the horrors of our century.

The Greek gods are not good gods because they mirror – and mirror accurately not wishfully – who we are. The Greek religion is not a religion of serene, perfected being but of tumultuous becoming: sensual, emotional, impulsive. It is significant that Homer places the gods not in heaven, in a psychological outerspace, but on Olympos – on top of a mountain but still firmly attached to the earth. And the Greeks could both revere them and laugh with them; and the gods would laugh back.

In Greek the word for sin (*armartia*) means simply missing the mark. There is no haunting connotation of moral judgement, no sense of departing from the path of righteousness and, therefore, no need for guilt and remorse but only for correction. But by the time Plato was writing the *Republic*, the tendency to reduce the mystery and paradoxes of a living religion to a coherent system of philosophy and ethics was gathering force:

> Neither, then, said I, must we believe this, or suffer it to be said, that Theseus, the son of Poseidon, and Pirithous, the son of Zeus, attempted such dreadful rapes, nor that any other child of a god or hero would have brought himself to accomplish the terrible and impious deeds that they now falsely relate of them. But we must constrain the poets either to deny that these are their deeds or that they are the children of gods, but not to make both statements or attempt to persuade our youth that the gods are the begetters of evil, and that heroes are no better than men. For, as we were saying, such utterances are both impious and false. For we proved, I take it, that for evil to arise from gods is an impossibility. And they are furthermore harmful to those that hear them. For every man will be very lenient with his own misdeeds if he is convinced that such are and were the actions of 'the near-sown seed of gods'.

This is the classic statement of the social function of religion: religion as one of the pillars of a sound and stable society. But this is not the religion of the Greek gods. Their religion was summed up in the inscription on Apollo's temple at Delphi: 'Know thyself'. Know thyself as you are *and* as you are becoming, in your failings and destructive impulses no less than in your glory and essential divinity. This is religion as Thomas Mann experienced it: 'as the opposite of negligence and disregard, as taking care, respecting, considering, as a *vigilant* attitude, and finally as a concerned, attentive receptivity to the movements of the universal spirit'. This is the religion of attending to all the gods in all their aspects: a shift of perspective away from the personal and transient, towards the universal, the eternally recurring, the ageless, the mythological.

The gods do not tell us how to live. They are neither moral nor immoral, neither teachers nor examples. They simply provide an invisible background against which our lives take on new depth and meaning. 'As metaphors speak with inverted commas, giving an echo to a plain word, so when we begin to mythologize our plain lives they gain another dimension. We are more distanced because we are more richly involved.'

'We dance round in a ring and suppose,
But the Secret sits in the middle and knows'   ROBERT FROST

Greek religion was a rich mixture of external forms, festivals, ceremonies, sacrifices and of inner experiences, mysteries, rites, initiations. While most men stood around in a ring and supposed, content with an external participation in festivals and ceremonies, many longed to unite with the Secret that sat in the middle and knew. For Aristotle, the highest thing a man could aspire to was the intellectual contemplation of god, which led to wisdom. But for those who sought union with god, intellectual contemplation was not enough. Nor were ceremonies and sacrifices enough. The official religion of the city-states and Homer's religion, with their emphasis on the gulf between men and gods, did not satisfy man's craving to connect with his inherent divinity. It was the Eleusinian Mysteries and the Orphic religion that placed this craving at the centre of man's life.

Orpheus, the legendary singer who inspired generations of European poets, was the original source of the Orphic religion with its emphasis on man's cultivation of his divine nature, on personal responsibility, on purity and goodness, on living what Plato calls an 'Orphic' life, with one's whole being turned towards the reality that lies on the other side of all conflict. Central to the Orphic religion was a belief in reincarnation which paralleled Plato's account in the *Republic*. All souls destined for rebirth were required to drink from the waters of Lethe, of Forgetfulness, so that before their return to Earth a memory veil would drop over everything they had experienced since their death. Only the souls that had attained their final incarnation and had 'flown out of the sorrowful, weary circle' were allowed to know and remember everything. This connection and ultimate union with the divine was the goal both of the Orphic and of the Eleusinian Mysteries. 'When a man has devoted himself to this', wrote Plato, 'and come to feel at home in it, there suddenly arises, as if kindled by a jumping spark, something like a fire in the soul, and from then it continues to feed itself.' And it continued to feed itself not only through initiations and purification rites but, most importantly, through everything that life brought, through living itself.

To persuade men to 'tend to their souls' and to connect them to a better way of living, you first had to give them, according to Socrates, a vision of the truth. This passion for truth, rather than the passion for beauty, was for Goethe the distinguishing mark of the Greeks. Nor was it a theoretical passion for an abstract truth. Man, Socrates was convinced, would choose the right if he only knew what it was. 'No one', he said, 'does wrong willingly.' So the passion for truth was a very practical passion informing the art of living that led to the realization of man's divine potential. In this context, the gods were transformed from forces that had to be propitiated in the course of an official religion to powerful symbols of the depth and complexity of man's experience. And the personification of the energies they represented made them powerful catalysts of self-knowledge and understanding.

'I dare do all that may become a man;
Who dares do more is none' MACBETH

What becomes a man and what oversteps the measure of humanity were questions that received no unanimous answer in Greek religious thought. 'The cleverness of men is no real wisdom', cries the chorus in Euripides' *Bacchae*, 'if it means forgetting their mortality.' 'All hail! I go about among you an immortal god, no longer a mortal!' asserts the philosopher Empedocles in an exultant outburst that many in ancient Greece would have regarded as a clear case of hubris – of human insolence attempting to breach the gulf between gods and men. Such attempts, poets and playwrights warned, were destined to end in disaster.

'Men?' wrote the poet Simonides of Keos, 'Small is their strength, fruitless their cares, brief their life, toil upon toil. Death inescapable hangs over all alike, dealing impartially with good and bad.' Set against this view of man's nature and man's lot, that drew much strength from Homer, was the belief, growing more widespread after the fifth century, that man's aim was, in Plato's words, 'the completest possible assimilation to God'. Yet the two views are much less incompatible than it has so far been assumed. 'I am a weak, ephemeral creature', wrote Kazantzakis, 'made of mud and dream. But I feel all the powers of the universe within me.' Man is indeed guilty of hubris and of overstepping his measure to the extent that he sets himself in competition with the gods, compulsively seeking to prove his greatness while ignoring its true source in his own connection with the divine. In fact the heroic rebellion against the gods is in essence an adolescent rebellion against our own unrealized divinity, a proud, misguided assertion of the established consciousness against the infinitely greater possibilities that man encompasses.

> Man, proud man,
> Drest in a little brief authority, –
> Most ignorant of what he's most assured,
> His glassy essence, – like an angry ape,
> Plays such fantastic tricks before high heaven
> As make the angels weep.

When Plato asserted that 'God is the measure' and Protagoras objected that 'Man is the measure', the conflict between two fundamentally different attitudes to man and to life was given a classic expression that continues to permeate our time. Yet there is reconciliation possible between the two measures, a reconciliation that eliminates the element of hubris from Protagoras' statement. God is undoubtedly the invisible measure, infinitely more powerful than man's visible, realized greatness. But man can and does become the measure of things to the extent that he is awakened to his invisible, divine nature and manifests in his life the divine truth that he incarnates.

'I grasp nothing in the life of the gods so much as the moment in which they withdraw themselves: what would be a God without the cloud which preserves him? What would be a worn-out God?' RAINER MARIA RILKE

Rilke's statement makes perfect sense to our modern, Cartesian mind that has placed concepts before experiences, but it would have made no sense to the Greeks. The language of gods withdrawing in order to recharge themselves is the language of rationalism, and whether in the fifth century BC or the twentieth century AD, rationalism could never encompass the reality of the gods. For the Greeks there was no place, no act, no moment when the gods were not. 'The gods could not absent themselves from existence in a Protestant theological manner; they *were* existence. There could not be two worlds – one sacred, one profane; one Christ's, one Caesar's – for the mundane was precisely the scene of divine enactment.'

To understand the meaning of the gods for the Greeks and their meaning for our lives, we have to recapture the mythic way of seeing, where 'once upon a time' is now and forever and where the gods are inexhaustible symbols that cannot be reduced to allegories and poetic inventions. Herder said that 'poets and none but poets made the myths and gave them their character', but in truth poets have as much to do with the creation of myths as we do with the creation of our dreams. Our dreams *happen* to us and the myths are just as spontaneous a manifestation of the mysterious play of the human spirit. The manifestation is spontaneous but, far from being arbitrary, it is primordial and universal. Through the gods and their myths our lives are taken out of their blinding immediacy and placed in 'a momentary eternity which encloses everything, past and future'. As we feel our way through a twilight of self-knowledge, our different personalities and the roles we play, normally fragmentary and inconsistent, can find in the different gods a voice and a universal expression that recognizes their autonomous influence in our lives, as potent as it is invisible.

'Whoever will look narrowly into his own bosom', wrote Montaigne, 'will hardly find himself twice in the same condition. I give to my soul sometimes one face and sometimes another . . . all the contrarieties are there to be found in one corner or another. . . . I have nothing to say of myself entirely, simply, and solidly without mixture and confusion.' Jung called this babble of inner voices 'the little people', who draw their power from the universal figures, the gods we carry within us – ultimately far more important in steering our fate than our well-defined, socially recognized 'I'.

The many voices in us have different gods to obey, different moments of coming to the forefront and withdrawing to the background. Recognizing the different gods in us dissolves our exclusive identification with the 'I' of our surface personality and at the same time expands the scope of our being to include an entire mythical universe. Jung actually described his mode of psychological thinking as 'mythologizing', and even Freud, whose aim was to create a scientific psychology, found that concepts could not begin to express his psychological insights and ended up creating what Wittgenstein called 'a powerful mythology'. He also ended up receiving not the Nobel Prize for Science but the Goethe Prize for Literature. Scientific concepts can help us sort out and grasp objects and things, but when it comes to ourselves and our lives we need the language of myths – emotional, dramatic, sensual – that can embrace the battles among the gods being waged in our souls and evoke a universal significance in the roles we play and the problems and games in which we are caught.

When, like the ancients, we search for the gods in the events of our lives, in our feelings, attitudes and motives, we find not only a hidden richness in our internal confusions but a structure of meaning underlying our raw experiences, turning our lives into an unending inner adventure full of creative possibilities. 'But what can a man "create" if he doesn't happen to be a poet? . . . If you have nothing at all to create, then perhaps you create yourself.' And imagination is a true creative power from which destiny itself is bodied forth.

'It is, of course, the stars and the bodies we can perceive existing along with them that must be named first as the visible gods, and the greatest, most worshipful, and clearsighted of them all' PLATO

Plato called the stars and planets the visible gods, and in the *Republic* what happens to souls and to the stars turns on the same spindle of Necessity. Plato's fascination was with astrology as psychology – with the connection between the movements of men on earth and the motions of planets in the heavens and with the essential correspondence of the planets to the psychic forces represented by the ancient gods and goddesses. 'The morning star, which is also the evening star, is usually reputed to be that of Aphrodite . . . and that which keeps pace at once with it and with the sun, the star of Hermes . . . the slowest moving of all is called that of Cronos, that which is next slowest we should call the star of Zeus, and the next slowest after him the star of Ares, and his has the ruddiest colour of them all.'

The gods' names have been changed since Plato's time to their Roman equivalents – Hermes to Mercury, Ares to Mars, Aphrodite to Venus, Zeus to Jupiter, Poseidon to Neptune – but what the ancients knew intuitively when they gave the planets their particular names has been borne out empirically in the connections between the nature of the gods and the nature of the planets.

> It is *not* that astrologers have over the years arbitrarily used the stories of the ancients about Venus, Mars and Mercury to project meaning onto the planets. ... On the contrary, astrologers seem to have been recognizing with striking intuitive and perceptive clarity that the planets named Venus, Mars and Mercury have tended to 'act' exactly as their mythical counterparts would lead us to expect they should.... To encounter the profound universal intelligence that establishes a systematic correspondence between a physical planet and a mythological essence which affects life processes in innumerable ways is to have one's benighted intellect drawn to a totally new understanding of life.

The term zodiac was first used by Aristotle in the fourth century BC. Since then, and especially in this century with its facile fascination with astrology, the meaning of the astrological horoscope has tended to be reduced to the celestial equivalent of reading the cards or the coffee beans: a quest for clues to our immutable fate. The perspective we gain from seeing the planets active in our lives in terms of the gods they embody transforms astrology from a way of gaining knowledge of our future to a way of gaining understanding of ourselves.

All signs and all planets are contained in each horoscope chart, in the same way that we contain in us all the gods. What is more, each of the signs of the zodiac and each of the gods has a light and a dark side. Jupiter can affect us either in the judging and punishing aspect of Zeus seeking tyrannical control over the flow of life or in his expansive, empowering aspect of the benevolent father. In the same way, Venus, so often symbolized by the dog in Greek mythology, is both the goddess of love and beauty and the love goddess turned into bitch, as Helen, Aphrodite's earthly embodiment, testifies in the *Iliad*.

The principle of opposites is present in each god and each planet – in their capacity to manifest their essential nature either positively or negatively. It is up to us to what extent it will be the constructive or the destructive aspect of each particular god or sign that will rule our life's expression.

In the starry vault of our lives each god is a constellation of different values and attitudes, passions and compulsions, fantasies and failures. In the sections that follow on the individual gods and goddesses we will look to Olympos to find in each god's essence patterns that reflect our own expressions and experiences. The aim is neither to paint portraits of the gods nor to write their biographies but to evoke the forces each god embodies – in all their brilliance and all their darkness.

RIGHT The acanthus, whose graceful leaves were the inspiration for the sculptured decorations of Corinthian columns. In the background is the Hephaisteion, dedicated to Hephaistos and Athena, in Athens.

PAGE 34 The milk from Hera's breasts, the ancients believed, made the Milky Way, and when a few drops fell on the ground, lilies sprang up on the spot – a symbol of fertility and the sacred flower of the goddess of marriage and childbirth.

PAGE 35 The asphodel, often found among ruins and in cemeteries, was, to the ancient Greeks, a symbol of death. The souls of men whom life had worn out, wrote Homer, dwelt in the 'meadows of asphodel' in the Underworld.

PAGE 36 Wild narcissi, named after the beautiful youth who fell in love with his own reflection and pined away, worn out by the hopelessness of his love.

PAGE 37 Wheat was sacred to Demeter in her Earth Mother aspect, and poppies were a symbol of her daughter Persephone, who personified intuition and inspiration.

THE GODS

PAGE 38 During the contest between Athena and Poseidon for control of Athens, the goddess struck the rocky and bare soil of the Acropolis with her spear and there suddenly sprang into being the olive tree – the symbol of peace that became the sacred tree of Athens and Athena.

PAGE 39 'Tell me is it the mad
pomegranate tree that greets
us afar
Tossing a leafy handkerchief of
cool fire . . .
Tell me, she who unfolds her
wings on the breasts of all
things
On the breast of our deepest
dreams, is it the mad
pomegranate tree?'
ODYSSEUS ELYTIS

LEFT Herakles' temple at Agrigento in Sicily. 'It is Herakles, the son of Zeus, that I will sing now, the greatest man that ever lived on earth! Alcmena gave him birth in Thebes with its beautiful places after she made love to that black cloud, Zeus.'
Homeric Hymn to Herakles

POSEIDON

RIDING HIS CHARIOT OF HORSES ACROSS THE SEA, Poseidon, god of the oceans and god of horses, embodies the two age-old symbols of the unconscious: horse and water. Water has always evoked in man the infinite mystery, infinite possibilities and infinite dangers of our fluid unconscious. With no predetermined shape of its own, it is constantly in movement, never changing yet never the same for two successive moments. And the horse personifies in its primitive potency the instinctive drives of our own raw nature. We have reined the horse, we have controlled or submerged our instincts, but the longing in us to be united with our life-giving power remains unquenchable.

'Equus, I love you', cries the young boy in Peter Shaffer's play. 'Now! – Bear me away! Make us one person!' And the psychiatrist in the play recognizes the same longing in himself. 'You see, I'm wearing that horse's head myself. That's the feeling. All reined up in old language and old assumptions, straining to jump clean-hoofed on to a whole new track of being I only suspect is there. I can't see it, because my educated, average head is being held at the wrong angle. I can't jump because the bit forbids it, and my own basic force – my horsepower, if you like – is too little.'

Our horsepower does become too little when our cultured, educated heads reject the unconscious powers over which Poseidon rules. But the fear that leads us to suppress them is a very real one. Poseidon was the most primitive of the gods, the earthshaker, the god of storms and earthquakes, of the sudden devastation of tidal waves – the dangers unleashed when the forces slumbering under the surface of consciousness erupt.

Poseidon's menacing nature and suppressed savagery find countless expressions in his myths. Angered at Troy, he sends against the city a sea-monster that would break to the surface of the water and devour everything

Marble statue of Poseidon, Roman copy of a Greek original, from Cherchel in Algeria. Homer called the god of the oceans and of horses 'the illustrious shaker of the earth'. Underneath his majestic, self-contained dignity the god of storms and earthquakes embodies the infinite possibilities of our fluid unconscious but also its turbulence and the dangers unleashed when the forces slumbering under the surface of consciousness erupt.

POSEIDON

Marble slab from the eastern frieze of the
Parthenon showing (from left to right)
Poseidon, Apollo and Artemis,
c.442–438 BC.
'Once more let it be your morning, Gods.
We repeat. You alone are primal source
With you the world arises, and a fresh start
    gleams
On all the fragments of our failures. . . .'
RAINER MARIA RILKE

and everyone on the Trojan plain; seeking revenge for the blinding of the Cyclopes, he sends a torrential storm to wreck the raft Odysseus has built to escape from Calypso's island; furious with Queen Cassiopeia for boasting that she was even more beautiful than the goddesses of the sea, he sends a savage beast to lay waste her kingdom of Ethiopia.

Monsters and storms are powerful symbols of the turbulence and the dangers of the unconscious. And what Poseidon's myths tell us is that the hero who will save us from its dangers has to dive into the monster, plunge into the sea and, having confronted its dangers, discover its mysteriously creative source and the power of renewal, personified in the myths by a beautiful princess. Troy was saved by Herakles who dived into the monster and came out through its belly, leaving it dead and releasing Hesione, the daughter of the king. Odysseus was saved after swimming in the ocean, the deep, dark, night sea of the soul, for two days and two nights, until he reached the island of the Phaeacians, and found on the shore the little princess Nausicaa. And Andromeda, Queen Cassiopeia's daughter, who had been offered as a propitiatory sacrifice to the god, was saved by Perseus; he dived at the monster and killed it just as, its huge jaws wide open, it was ready to swallow the chained Andromeda.

The beautiful princesses, like the Rhinemaidens' gold glinting beneath the waters in Wagner's *Ring*, represent the supreme value, the creative force, submerged in the subconscious, which is why Poseidon is both the 'loud-crushing Earthshaker' and 'the god of the creative flow'. In many of his myths the emblem of his ferocious power, the trident, is transformed into an agent of creation and generation. He would strike the trident on rocks or dry land and a spring of fresh running water would be released where there was none before. Life and creativity come forth from the same unconscious source that can bring about destruction and dissolution. 'Why did they make birds so delicate and fine as those sea-swallows when the ocean can be so cruel?', asks Hemingway in *The Old Man and The Sea*. 'The old man always thought of the sea as *la mar*, which is what people call her in Spanish when they love her. Some of the younger fishermen ... spoke of her as *el mar* which is masculine. They spoke of her as a contestant or a place or even an enemy. But the old man always thought of her as feminine and as something that gave or withheld great favours. . . .'

The paradoxical nature of the sea is the paradoxical nature of its god: he is both the avenger and the protector of those at sea. In ancient times navigation of the oceans was a highly risky and dangerous undertaking and, at all times, the journey into the darkness and uncertainty of the unconscious is fraught with the dangers of disintegration. Yet in the same way that venturing into the oceans is essential for survival, venturing into the

PAGE 48 Head of the famous
bronze statue generally thought
to represent Poseidon, found in
the sea off Cape Artemision,
c. 460 BC.

PAGE 49 Mt Phengari, on the
island of Samothrace, from
where, Homer tells us in the
Iliad, Poseidon watched the
battle of Troy: 'Neither did the
powerful shaker of the earth
keep blind watch; for he sat and
admired the fighting and the run
of the battle, aloft on the top of
the highest summit of timbered
Samos, the Thracian place; and
from there all Ida appeared
before him, and the city of
Priam was plain to see, and the
ships of the Achaians. There he
came up out of the water, and
sat, and pitied the Achaians who
were beaten by the Trojans, and
blamed Zeus for it in bitterness.'

unconscious is essential for life. 'The connection with the suprapersonal or collective unconscious', wrote Jung, 'means an extension of man beyond himself . . . a rebirth in a new dimension as was literally enacted in certain of the ancient mysteries. . . . We can no longer deny that the dark stirrings of the unconscious are active powers, that psychic forces exist which cannot be fitted into our rational order. . . . The layman can hardly conceive how much his inclinations, moods and decisions are influenced by the dark forces of his psyche, and how dangerous or helpful they may be in shaping his destiny.'

This ambivalence is represented in astrological symbolism by the planet Neptune that is said to 'rule' the Twelfth House dealing with the depths of the soul from which come both the oceanic experience of oneness with life and the danger of losing oneself in the ocean of the unconscious, in its vastness and formlessness. Astrologers have associated Neptune with poetry and music, feeling and imagination, and the discovery of the planet in 1846 coincided with the height of the Romantic era. In its positive aspect Neptune leads to the urge to devote ourselves to goals that transcend selfish pursuits and focus instead on the service of the larger whole – the family, the community, the world. It can also come to the fore in the quest for mystical experiences and idealized love and in our absorption in art and religion. In its negative aspect it can bring about instability, the urge to escape from the responsibilities of reality into day-dreams, infantile fantasies or drugs, an obsessive religiosity, or a fanatical pursuit of utopian politics where the idealized ends are used to justify the most cruel means.

The extreme ambivalence of the planet and of the god is embodied in Poseidon's son Proteus who has the power to take on any number of shapes and forms. He can transform himself into a lion, a serpent, a panther, a boar, running water, a leafy tree. . . . Transformation is the essence of the journey into the unconscious and of the extension of man beyond mundane reality and his narrow self. The instinct that drives us to constant change and transformation, however great the dangers and powerful the monsters we encounter along the way, is the instinct that Poseidon personifies – the instinct that drives us to wander through endless adventures, as Odysseus was forced to do by the sea god, until we reach Ithaca, the place where we started from, and, through transformed eyes, see it again for the first time.

LEFT Poseidon ruled over 'all the creatures of the sea', menacing and benign. The sea-monsters that appear in the god's myths are powerful symbols of the turbulence and the dangers of the unconscious.

ABOVE Triton, Poseidon's son, half-fish, half-human in shape, was a satyr of the sea, raping men and women and spreading terror wherever he appeared. Floor mosaic, c. 200 BC.

APOLLO

I am the eye with which the Universe
    Beholds itself and knows itself divine;
All harmony of instrument or verse,
    All prophecy, all medicine is mine,
All light of art or nature; – to my song
Victory and praise in their own right belong.

FOR SHELLEY, APOLLO WAS 'the eye with which the Universe beholds itself'. For William Rose Benét, 'all creation's growth and flowering swelled Apollo's theme. Myriad-toned of pandemonium, scaled from lion to bee, all of brute creation's psalmody found its consonant key.' For Hölderlin, through the young, enchanting sun god, 'life and the spirit catch fire in us'. For Byron, Apollo was 'the God of life, and poesy, and light – the Sun in human limbs array'd'. For Swinburne, he was 'the word, the light, the life, the breath, the glory'.

Apollo is Western man's ideal of man. When Hamlet extols his vision of man, he is extolling Apollo: 'What a piece of work is a man! How noble in reason! how infinite in faculty! in form, in moving, how express and admirable! in action how like an angel! in apprehension how like a god! the beauty of the world!' Reason, nobility, form, action, apprehension, beauty, are all Apollo's essential attributes.

He embodies the Western ideal of beauty and form in its classical perfection. In Giraudoux's play, *The Apollo of Bellac*, the 'Man from Bellac' conjures up the god of beauty:

I am taller than mortal man. My head is small and fringed with golden ringlets. From the line of my shoulders, the geometricians derived the idea of the square. From my eyebrows the bowman drew the concept of the arc. I am

The 'Apollo of the Tiber River', Roman copy of a Greek original of the 5th century BC, found in the Tiber.

53

nude and this nudity inspired in the musicians the idea of harmony. . . . As for the eyes, it's well you don't see them. The eyes of beauty are implacable. My eyeballs are silver. My pupils are graphite. From the eyes of beauty poets derived the idea of death. But the feet of beauty are enchanting. They are not feet that touch the ground. They are never soiled and never captive. The toes are slender, and from them artists derived the idea of symmetry.

Our longing for beauty is one of our strongest bonds to Apollo. 'Every man,' says the Apollo of Bellac, 'even the ugliest, feels in his heart a secret alliance with beauty. When you tell him he's handsome, he will simply hear outwardly the voice he has been listening to inwardly all his life. And those who believe it the least will be the most grateful. No matter how ugly they may have thought themselves, the moment they find a woman who thinks them handsome, they grapple her to their hearts with hooks of steel. For them, she is the princess of an enchanted world, the magic glass of truth.'

Our equally strong longing for order and harmony is another powerful bond to Apollo. The bringing of harmony into the boundless confusion, the discovery of order in the chaos, are both Apollo's gifts. 'Know thyself' and 'Nothing in excess' are the great precepts he has bequeathed humanity and by which the Western world has, with varying degrees of success, tried to live. Moderation has been enshrined as a principle both in our personal and in our collective morality. As for the Apollonian plea for self-knowledge, it has been interpreted both on the surface and in depth. In depth, it gives man a glimpse of the ultimately divine nature of the self; on the surface it becomes the perfect opening for commencement addresses and solemn editorials. 'This above all: to thine own self be true.' It is a principle to which we feel obliged to pay lip-service even when our behaviour denies it and our actions contradict it.

The spiritual force that Apollo embodies is at the foundation of our civilization: 'It proclaims the presence of the divine, not in the miracles of a supernatural power, not in the rigour of an absolute justice, not in the providence of an infinite love, but in the victorious splendour of clarity, in the intelligent sway of order and moderation.' As if to dramatize the contrast between Apollo's clarity and balance and the irrational and awesome power of raw nature, the abstract mathematical order of his temples was always set against the primordial wildness of the earth – it shone forth from it, yet was touched and complemented by it.

In their highest Apollonian expression, clarity, discipline and reason were steeped in spirit. He was, after all, the god of music and prophecy as well as the god of archery and heroic excellence. His arrows hit and killed; his lyre revealed the harmony of the spiritual order underlying reality: 'The tones of music act as the rays of the sun which throw everything into the harmonious light of the higher order.' And prophecy springs from a much deeper source than reason. The Pythia, Apollo's priestess at Delphi, had to fall into a trance before she could commune with the god and answer the questions put to the Delphic Oracle. She descended into the innermost vault of the temple, filled with the fumes of burned barley, hemp and laurel leaves, and her answers were so obscure and even incoherent that the god of clarity and light, the god the Greeks called Phoebus (bright, shining), was also known as Loxias, 'the ambiguous one'.

The priestess took her name from Python, the snake-dragon killed by Apollo. In one version of the myth, the stench from the dragon's decaying body rose from the depths and filled Pythia, inspiring her to prophecy, in the same way that the blood of the snake-dragon that Siegfried kills in Wagner's *Ring* teaches him the speech of the birds. The symbolism is unmistakable. The earthly powers cannot be suppressed, nor can their mystery be denied recognition. Clarity and reason may hold sway in Apollo's world but, for their full expression, they remain dependent on the secret knowledge and insight of the elemental depths in which all being is grounded.

The union of Apollo and Dionysos at Delphi was a divine acknowledgement of this. Despite the sharp opposition between their two realms, the two brothers were joined together by an eternal bond. 'In Apollo all of the splendour of the Olympic converges and confronts the realms of eternal becoming and eternal passing. Apollo with Dionysos, the intoxicated leader of the choral dance of the terrestrial sphere – that would give the total world dimension. In this union the Dionysiac earthly duality would be elevated into a new and higher duality, the eternal contrast between a restless, whirling life and a still, far-seeing spirit.' And the Apollonian spirit would reach its noblest heights. Not only did Apollo cede Delphi to Dionysos during the winter months but, as Plutarch tells us, they both received high honours throughout the year. Indeed the pediments of Apollo's temple portray on one side Apollo with Leto, his mother, Artemis and the Muses, and on the other side Dionysos with his raving Maenads.

Even Apollo's handmaidens, the Muses, the daughters of Zeus and Mnemosyne, are personifications of man's highest intellectual and artistic aspirations and bear testimony to the essential interconnectedness of reason and intuition, clarity and vision. 'Our earliest education', says Plato in the *Laws*, 'comes through the Muses and Apollo.' And the nine Muses – or simply 'the Nine' as poets through the ages have called them – were the source of inspiration for scientists and historians, no less than for poets and artists. Urania was the Muse of astronomy and astrology; Clio, the Muse of history; Melpomene, the Muse of tragedy; Thalia, the Muse of comedy; Terpsichore, the Muse of choral song; Calliope, the Muse of epic poetry;

Erato, the Muse of love poetry; Euterpe, the Muse of lyric poetry; and Polyhymnia, the Muse of sacred poetry.

> Did the stars and the tides and your own heart
> Dance with the heavenly Nine?

Apollo may have been a distant god, but there was nothing distant about the Muses: men's hearts danced with them, men's minds were inspired by them, men's souls melted and their spirits soared through them. Apollo's handmaidens wrought their effect on men in a way which was clearly Dionysian.

Despite the mythological union of the two gods, the contrast between Apollonian objective clarity and Dionysian mystic exuberance remains a psychological reality that has dominated Western history. Apollo may have been the god of the arts as well as science, of music and poetry as well as mathematics and medicine, but in our culture the split between the scientific and the unscientific, the objective and the subjective, has become absolute. Yet as all the great scientists would attest, there is nothing exclusively rational and objective about science. Imagination, intuition, inspiration, enthusiasm – all the Dionysian elements of our being – are at least as important in scientific discovery as Apollonian logic, discipline and clarity.

When Descartes announced 'I think, therefore I am', and modern man rejected the Dionysian element in the Apollonian order, our culture became fatally fragmented. What was not 'objective' was automatically assumed to be untrue, reason's march of conquest became a rout, and man, the self-reliant victor, was transformed into our century's uprooted, haunted fugitive. The god of light and reason, disconnected from Dionysos and the depths, became exhausted, and the exhaustion has spread over our Apollonian world.

> Apollo from his shrine
> Can no more divine
> With hollow shriek the steep of Delphos leaving. . . .

> The languid strings do scarcely move!
> The sound is forc'd, the notes are few!

Plato called Apollo a scholar in the school of love, but love was the area in which the god of reason was least at home. The myths of his adventures with women are dominated by unsuccessful chases and fleeing maidens. In contrast with Apollo's failures, Dionysos magnetizes the feminine, 'drawing it forth like the sap in plants, the wine, and the milk that flows at his birth'.

Apollo's first love was Daphne, the daughter of the river god Peneus:

The Muse, Roman copy of a Greek original from the first half of the 2nd century BC. Apollo may have been a distant god, but there was nothing distant about his nine Muses: men's hearts danced with them, men's minds were inspired by them, men's souls melted and their spirits soared through them.

Apollo loved her, and longed to obtain her; and he who gives oracles to all the world was not wise enough to look into his own fortunes. He saw her hair flung loose over her shoulders, and said, 'If so charming in disorder, what would it be if arranged?' He saw her eyes bright as stars; he saw her lips, and was not satisfied with only seeing them. He admired her hands and arms, naked to the shoulder, and whatever was hidden from view he imagined more beautiful still. He followed her; she fled, swifter than the wind, and delayed not a moment at his entreaties. 'Stay,' said he, 'daughter of Peneus; I am not a foe. Do not fly me as a lamb flies the wolf, or a dove the hawk. It is for love I pursue you. You make me miserable, for fear you should fall and hurt yourself on these stones, and I should be the cause. Pray run slower, and I will follow slower. I am no clown, no rude peasant. Jupiter is my father, and I am lord of Delphos and Tenedos, and know all things, present and future. I am the god of song and the lyre. My arrows fly true to the mark; but, alas! an arrow more fatal than mine has pierced my heart! I am the god of medicine, and know the virtues of all healing plants. Alas! I suffer a malady that no balm can cure!'

The nymph continued her flight, and left his plea half uttered. And even as she fled she charmed him. The wind blew her garments, and her unbound hair streamed loose behind her. The god grew impatient to find his wooings thrown away, and, sped by Cupid, gained upon her in the race. It was like a hound pursuing a hare, with open jaws ready to seize, while the feebler animal darts forward, slipping from the very grasp. So flew the god and the virgin — he on the wings of love, and she on those of fear. The pursuer is the more rapid, however, and gains upon her, and his panting breath blows upon her hair. Her strength begins to fail, and ready to sink, she calls upon her father, the river god: 'Help me, Peneus! open the earth to enclose me, or change my form, which has brought me into this danger!'

Scarcely had she spoken, when a stiffness seized all her limbs; her bosom began to be enclosed in a tender bark; her hair became leaves; her arms became branches; her foot stuck fast in the ground, as a root; her face became a tree-top, retaining nothing of its former self but its beauty. Apollo stood amazed. He touched the stem, and felt the flesh tremble under the new bark. He embraced the branches, and lavished kisses on the wood. The branches shrank from his lips. 'Since you cannot be my wife,' said he, 'you shall assuredly be my tree. I will wear you for my crown; I will decorate with you my harp and my quiver; and when the great Roman conquerors lead up the triumphal pomp to the Capitol, you shall be woven into wreaths for their brows. And, as eternal youth is mine, you also shall be always green, and your leaf know no decay.' The nymph, now changed into a Laurel tree, bowed its head in grateful acknowledgement.

'He caught at love and filled his arms with bays.' The next time Apollo 'caught at love', he sought to get love back by promising to teach Cassandra the art of prophecy. He kept his promise, but Cassandra still refused to be his lover. Divine gifts, once given, cannot be withdrawn, so Apollo's revenge was that she could keep her gift of prophecy but that no one would believe her. Cassandra, one of the daughters of the king of Troy, had to suffer the terrible fate of always knowing when disaster threatened and never being able to persuade her people of what she knew. Even when she cried out that Greeks were hidden in the wooden horse, no one gave her words a thought. In the end her own father, convinced that she had gone mad, had her shut away and guarded. When Troy fell, she was given to Agamemnon and met a brutal end at Clytemnestra's hands when they reached Mycenae.

Sibyl was another young woman Apollo loved. Once again it was a love that was not returned, and once again Apollo took his revenge. In Ovid's *Metamorphoses*, Sibyl, with a deep sigh, tells her story to Aeneas, whom she had guided in his passage through the Underworld:

> When I was still an innocent young girl, I was offered endless, eternal life, if I would yield myself to Phoebus, who was in love with me. While the god hoped for my consent, he was eager to bribe me with gifts and said: 'Maiden of Cumae, choose what you wish, and you will have your desire!' I pointed to a heap of dust which had been swept together, and foolishly asked that I might have as many birthdays as there were grains of dust; but I forgot to ask for perpetual youth as well. Yet Phoebus offered me all those years, and eternal youth too, if I would suffer his love. I scorned his gift, and remained unwed. Now the happier time of life is fled, and with shaky steps comes sick old age, which I must long endure. For, as you see me now, I have lived through seven generations; in order to equal the number of grains of dust, it remains for me to see three hundred harvests, three hundred vintages. A time will come when I shall shrink from my present fine stature into a tiny creature, thanks to my length of days, and my limbs, shrivelled with age, will be reduced to a mere handful. No one will think that I was ever loved, or that I pleased a god, and perhaps even Phoebus himself will fail to recognize me, or else deny that he ever had any affection for me. So changed shall I be, and invisible to anyone. But still, the fates will leave me my voice, and by my voice I shall be known.

Sibyl shrivels up into a disembodied voice, Daphne turns into a tree, Cassandra prophesies but fails to touch those who hear her. The god who embodies light and truth and beauty wreaks destruction in the world of love and the feminine. The dominance of an exclusive masculinity, detached and dispassionate, is Apollo's dark side. 'The man is the source of life', the god proclaims in the *Eumenides*. Dionysos encompasses the feminine in himself; Apollo is disconnected from it. He embodies the will to power that, cut off from the feminine, from love and intuition, has brought about our shrivelled-up rationalist order, with its naive belief in the absolute manageability of life and of human beings. This will to power was the

LEFT Head of Apollo on a silver coin, 392–358 BC.
'Not one touch of our low lives'
  baseness,
Not one stain of our sordid
  strife,
Mars the peace of thy cloudless
  forehead,
Blurs the calm of thy conquering
  life.' JOHN COWPER POWYS

RIGHT Apollo's temple at Corinth. Only seven monolithic columns remain from this temple which was built in the mid 6th century BC and is one of the oldest in Greece.

PAGE 62 The theatre and, beyond, Apollo's temple at Delphi. Despite the sharp opposition between their two realms, Apollo, the god of reason and moderation, and Dionysos, the god of ecstasy and the theatre, were joined together at Delphi.

PAGE 63 The Charioteer at Delphi, c. 488 BC.
'Let me compare the soul to a pair of winged horses and a charioteer. . . . Our human charioteer drives his in a pair; and one of them is noble and of noble breed, and the other is ignoble and of ignoble breed; and the driving of them is hard and difficult. . . .'

PLATO, *Phaedrus*

dominant theme of Apollo's adolescence. He had to suffer for it by being forced to serve a mortal man, King Admetus, as a herdsman. This was the penalty imposed by Zeus on the young god for killing the Cyclopes who had forged Zeus' thunderbolts. Apollo's punishment lasted a year. Our culture's wilful phase of adolescence is still going on and so are the punishments that go with it.

But life is revolting against the will to control and dominate, against rationalist smugness and cold abstractions. 'Knowledge is not wisdom,' cries the chorus in the *Bacchae*. 'Thoughts too long make life short.' If there is one lesson our century has taught us, it is that it is irrational not to recognize the irrational, and dangerous and destructive as well. When the Apollonian *know thyself* is united with the Dionysian *be thyself*, when reason is reintegrated with our stubbornly neglected spirit and intuition, then we will have achieved the wholeness in which lies healing and renewal. It was a wholeness achieved at Delphi through the intimate union of the two gods – a powerful symbol of our culture's most urgent need.

ABOVE Apollo's temple at Didyma near Miletos in Turkey. There was an ancient oracle-shrine to Apollo going back to the Archaic period on this site, and the Archaic lion in the foreground was originally part of a group of statues of lions and priests which lined the sacred way leading to the temple from Miletos.

PAGE 66 Apollo, or possibly Eros, Roman copy of a Greek original of the 4th century BC. Entwined round the tree trunk is the monstrous serpent Python, who inhabited Delphi before the coming of Apollo.

RIGHT The Terrace of the Lions on the island of Delos where Apollo and his sister Artemis were born.

PAGE 67 Apollo, Roman copy of a Greek bronze of the mid 5th century BC.
'Or view the Lord of the unerring bow,
The God of life, and poesy, and light –
The Sun in human limbs array'd, and brow
All radiant from his triumph in the fight.' BYRON

ARTEMIS

ARTEMIS IS FREEDOM – WILD, UNTRAMMELLED, aloof from all entanglements. She is a huntress, a dancer, the goddess of nature and wildness, a virgin physically and, even more important, a virgin psychologically, inviolable, belonging to no one, defined by no relationship, confined by no bond.

She was born on the unpeopled island of Delos and she is much more at home with animals than with people, in her element in wild nature, uneasy in our everyday world. The wild quail is her bird, the wild fig her fruit. She is Apollo's twin, the daughter of Leto and Zeus, and the myth of her birth immediately establishes her power and self-sufficiency. She is born first, easily, with no travail and, barely a few moments old, she becomes her mother's midwife, assisting over nine agonizing days and nights at the birth of her brother.

The longing for freedom is the essential Artemisian passion. When her father asks her, at the age of three, what gifts she most desires, she answers unhesitatingly: 'Pray, give me eternal virginity.' She also asks Zeus to give her as companions and playmates sixty daughters of Okeanos, all nine-year-olds. This was the age when girls entered the adolescent stage, the equivalent of the teenage years in our own culture. And Artemis is the primordial teenager who never moves beyond the adolescent stage into full womanhood. The nine-year-olds who left their mothers to enter the goddess' service stayed with her until it was time for them to marry and have their own children. They grew up and left; the goddess remained. Her own independence was her essential reality, not a transitional stage. Artemis' little handmaidens were called *arktoi*, 'female bears', and the celebration of their service to the goddess and this stage in their lives was called 'bearhood'. Yet there was nothing tomboyish about the strength that Artemis and her

Apollo and Artemis stride forward together during the battle between the gods and the giants, from the north frieze of the Siphnian Treasury at Delphi, *c*. 525 BC. Apollo and his twin sister Artemis are the eternal adolescents. The longing for freedom is the essential Artemisian urge; the longing for clarity, the essential Apollonian passion. They are both distant gods, detached and aloof, at a loss in the world of love, commitment and deep relationships.

hunting companions exuded. 'In the figure of the great huntress the little human bears met a new aspect of their feminine nature. It was a meeting with something wild and vigorous. . . .' It was also a meeting that had about it the aura of a mystery initiation – initiation into their own untamed nature and its power.

Today's Artemis women exude this freedom and vigour in the way they dress and move, in the way they look and behave. Aphrodite's curves have either disappeared into an androgynous figure or been squeezed into jeans and leotards. Artemis asked her father for a short hunting dress: 'so that I can kill wild animals'. Today's Artemis, vital and youthful at any age, is prepared to sacrifice elegance and sensuality in her clothes for freedom and movement. The goddess of the hunt has become the goddess of sports, aerobics and dancing, and sedentary femininity has been replaced by energetic activity.

Walter Otto has given the classic description of Artemis' paradoxical being:

> It is the crystal-clear being whose roots are still hidden in animal nature; the childlike-simple, yet unpredictable one; sweet lovability and diamond hardness. . . . She is the dancer and huntress, who takes the bear cub on her lap and runs races with the deer, death-bringing when she bends her bow, strange and unapproachable, like untamed nature, who is yet, like nature, wholly magic, living impulse, and sparkling beauty.

There is passion behind Artemis' remoteness, but it is a passion directed not at relationships but at the search for one's self, one's soul, in solitude and separateness. When we experience the pull to privacy, the pull to be alone as an instinctual, animal need, it is Artemis who is working through us. And when this pull becomes destructive, a chill lack of feeling that cuts us off from any real human communication, it is Artemis' darkness that is showing through. It is the darkness embodied in the myth of Actaeon's death.

Actaeon, son of King Cadmus, was out with his companions hunting the stag in the mountains when he stopped at a grotto enclosed with cypresses and pines to drink from the stream that was flowing through it. It was Artemis' favourite wild spot, and as Actaeon lifted his eyes from the stream he saw her bathing naked with her nymphs. Without hesitating for a moment, the goddess flung the water into the face of the intruder and transformed him into a stag. He began running and his own faithful hounds, cheered on by his huntsmen, turned on him and tore his heart out.

In William Rose Benét's poem, the ghost of Actaeon recollects the goddess' 'beauty beyond bearing':

Roman statue of the Ephesian Artemis among other museum pieces at Ephesus. Artemis was a huntress, a dancer, the goddess of nature and wilderness. But in Ephesus the statue of Mother Artemis with many breasts represented another aspect of the goddess who, though childless, was the protectress of childbirth. And the childbirths over which the goddess presides are both literal and spiritual. The 'mercurial queen of solitude' embodies the quest for a life that nourishes the soul struggling to be born in the middle of all our frenetic activity. It is the inner call of the soul that the goddess answers first and it is to the soul that she is Mother.

I was led by the willow,
I was haunted by the pool;
In the sunlit shallow
You shone white as wool;

You glowed alabaster
In the shadows of the stream;
The hounds of disaster
Bayed through dream.

Vase of light adored,
O the haughty throat,
Beauty like a sword
As you smote!

Glory unreturning –
Your eyes were so
Blazing, burning
On the foe.

I forget the legend,
I forget the pain;
The silvered sedge-end
Is the same.

Then beauty beyond bearing,
On an instant of amaze;
All the goddess flaring
From your gaze. . . .

The myth of Actaeon and Artemis, or Actaeon and Diana in Ovid's Latin version, inspired Titian, Rubens and Rembrandt and was turned into a metaphor by Shakespeare, Shelley, T. S. Eliot and Oscar Wilde. For Shelley, Actaeon's hounds are our own thoughts and emotions; we are their masters but cannot control them:

. . . . He, as I guess,
Had gazed on Nature's naked loveliness,
Actaeon-like, and now he fled astray
With feeble steps o'er the world's wilderness;
And his own Thoughts, along that rugged way
Pursued like raging hounds their father and their prey.

For Oscar Wilde, Actaeon is the modern man who has no reverence for the mystery of nature:

Methinks these new Actaeons boast too soon
    That they have spied on beauty; what if we
Have analysed the rainbow, robbed the moon
    Of her most ancient, chastest mystery,
Shall I, the last Endymion, lose all hope
Because rude eyes peer at my mistress through a telescope!

All these modern themes can be extracted from the ancient myth but, above all, it reveals dramatically the nature of the goddess. She is the goddess of distance, of inviolable boundaries, the goddess who 'must kill him who comes too close'. Here the demand for boundaries, for privacy, for time to be alone – all valid and vital needs – turns to outrage at the trespasser, to ruthlessness and the urge to punish. The huntress cannot bear to be turned into the hunted. So when Actaeon unwittingly transforms her into a passive object of desire she causes him to experience an even more drastic transformation: from hunter into victim. In Artemis' darkness there is no empathy, no allowance for motive and intention, no hesitation or second thoughts. She embodies the wildness both of nature and of human nature. It is a wildness that conceals great riches but its savagery cannot be evaded. The 'call of the wild' can either destroy or lead to the aliveness, the sense of freedom and vitality, that also belong to Artemis' realm.

> If you will contemplate your lack of fantasy, of inspiration and inner aliveness, which you feel as sheer stagnation and a barren wilderness, and impregnate it with the interest born of alarm at your inner death, then something can take shape in you, for your inner emptiness conceals just as great a fullness if only you will allow it to penetrate into you. If you prove receptive to this 'call of the wild', the longing for fulfilment will quicken the sterile wilderness of your soul as rain quickens the dry earth.

The call of the wild parallels the pull to solitude in Artemis' nature, both the hallowed solitude of untouched nature and the deep solitude that connects us to the untouched depths of soul. Listening to the inner call of the soul and of unexplored wilderness can bring an exhilarating sense of freedom – freedom from the mass of commonplace opinion, freedom from what binds us to the past, freedom from what is conventionally expected of us in the future. But there are no maps to guide us in the wilderness, and the modern men and women who have made Artemisian freedom the supreme value are, at the same time, living out the goddess' negative dimension: they cling to their freedom and independence until they are turned into estrangement and isolation. It is a very shallow view of freedom, though, that requires denial of commitment and deep relationship. Ultimately only by risking our freedom can we preserve and expand it. And then, instead of cutting ourselves off from life, trapped in the 'Amazon armour' of the goddess' wild followers, we can turn our freedom into an inner reality that survives in the midst of all outer entanglements. This is the freedom that denies no aspect of life, that releases our imagination and creativity and gives birth to all that is new.

In fact Artemis was not only the goddess of the hunt, the lover of solitary woods and the wild chase over the mountains, she was also 'the protectress of dewy youth' and, although childless, she was the protectress of childbirth. In Ephesus there was the famous statue of Mother Artemis with many breasts, and even into the Christian era, women in Greece and in Anatolia would pray to Artemis in time of childbirth. Indeed the last temple to the goddess was forcibly closed by the church as late as 500 AD. In Artemis' realm we are confronted both with the joys and with the pain of childbirth. And the childbirths over which the goddess presides are both literal and spiritual. The

LEFT Dying daughter of Niobe, *c.*450–440 BC.
'Niobe, she of the lovely tresses
. . . whose twelve children were
destroyed in her palace, six
daughters, and six sons in the
pride of their youth, whom
Apollo killed with arrows from
his silver bow, being angered
with Niobe, and shaft-
showering Artemis killed the
daughters; because Niobe
likened herself to Leto of the fair
colouring and said Leto had
borne only two, she herself had
borne many; but the two,
though they were only two,
destroyed all those others.'
HOMER, *Iliad*

PAGE 76 Artemis, Roman
copy of a Greek original. As a
young child on Zeus' knee,
Artemis asks her father for a
short hunting dress: 'So that I
can kill wild animals!'

PAGE 77 Artemis, Roman copy
of a Greek original, *c.*400 BC.
'And when she has hung up this
unstrung bow, when she has put
away her arrows, she puts over
her flesh a beautiful dress. Then
she begins the dances and their
sound is heavenly. . . .'
Homeric Hymn to Artemis

'mercurial queen of solitude' embodies the quest for a life that nourishes the soul struggling to be born in the middle of all our frenetic activity: 'Some fiercer caring demands this naked solitude for loam.'

There is fear in this radical confrontation with ourselves, not only fear of loneliness but also fear of what we may discover in these unexplored regions. And we long to escape into the arms of Aphrodite, lose ourselves in Hephaistos' workshop or prove our prowess through action and success in the world of Ares. But the solitary call of the soul cannot be stifled; only through it can we find the freedom that Artemis in her highest form embodies. 'Ask your soul', pleads Hermann Hesse in *My Belief*:

> Ask her who means freedom, whose name is love! Do not inquire of your intellect, do not search backwards through world history! Your soul will not blame you for having cared too little about politics, for having exerted yourself too little, hated your enemies too little, or too little fortified your frontiers. But she will perhaps blame you for so often having feared and fled from her demands, for never having had time to give her, your youngest and fairest child, no time to play with her, no time to listen to her song, for often having sold her for money, betrayed her for advancement. . . . You will be neurotic and a foe to life – so says your soul if you neglect me, and you will be destroyed if you do not turn to me with a wholly new love and concern.

And the protectress of all that is young, wild and vulnerable is also the protectress of our soul, the goddess who destroys us when other attachments distract us from the inner demands of our 'youngest and fairest child'.

APHRODITE

ALL GODDESSES ARE BEAUTIFUL BUT APHRODITE is the goddess of beauty. All goddesses love but Aphrodite is the love goddess. All gods and goddesses guide and inspire from within but Aphrodite possesses from within. She is 'a close god unable to keep her distance'. She invades our most secret places, she stirs yearnings more visceral and more consuming than any other god. Of all blessed gods and mortal men only the three Olympian virgins, Athena, Artemis and Hestia, are immune to her power. 'She even leads astray the mind of Zeus himself, the lover of lightning, the greatest of all . . . and when she wants to she can deceive that sage heart of his easily, and make him even mate with mortal women.' She embodies the wonder, the magic, the power of primordial femininity. 'Earth's archetypal Eve. All Womanhood.' She sinks men into the deepest morass of sensuality and lifts them to the exaltation of cosmic union.

Nowhere is this double nature of Aphrodite more beautifully portrayed than in the myth of the union of her son Eros with Psyche (Soul). The condition for their love was that they could unite only in darkness. When Psyche succumbs to her need to know, she lights a candle and in its light sees her lover in all his glory. 'Love cannot live with suspicion,' cries Eros and flies away. What is suspicion and curiosity at one level is, at another level, the soul's compulsion for light and consciousness, its unwillingness to be in a relationship shrouded in darkness. It is the beginning of a series of impossible tasks imposed on Psyche by Aphrodite before she can be reunited with her lost Eros – this time with no conditions. The final test is to enter the Underworld and there put into the box that Aphrodite has given her a drop of Persephone's beauty – the soul beauty of the depths. She fulfils the ultimate task and achieves the transformation of dark anonymous love into the love where the personal and the divine meet and merge. Psyche's

Marble statue of Aphrodite from Cyrene in Libya, Roman copy of a Hellenistic original, *c.* 100 BC. Aphrodite is the only goddess who glories in her nakedness, the only one to be portrayed nude in sculptures. She embodies sexuality free of ambivalence, anxieties and self-consciousness, a sexuality so natural and quintessential to her that no myth deals with her virginity or its loss.

marriage to Eros is the only wedding to take place in the presence of all the gods and goddesses on Olympos. And at the great feast that Zeus threw for the sacred union of Soul and Eros, Aphrodite danced.

She is the goddess both of the elemental mysteries of love and of its final revelation. Socrates was the first to give names to the two Aphrodites in the *Symposium*:

> No one, I think, will deny that there are two goddesses of that name – one, the elder, sprung from no mother's womb but from the heavens themselves, we call the Uranian, the heavenly Aphrodite, while the younger, daughter of Zeus and Dione, we call Pandemus, the earthly Aphrodite. It follows, then, that Love should be known as earthly or as heavenly according to the goddess in whose company his work is done.

Both goddesses, Socrates goes on to say, must command our homage. As Kenneth Clark writes, 'Perhaps no religion ever again incorporated physical passion so . . . naturally that all who saw her felt that the instincts they shared with the beasts they also shared with the gods.' In fact, even the Uranian Aphrodite is fully connected to the elements. She was born from the genitals of Uranus, cut off by his son Cronos and tossed into the sea. And she rose, full-grown, into life from the depths of the sea and the airy foam.

> And the Hours in their golden diadems
> received her with joy,
> clothed her in ambrosial garments,
> and placed a well-wrought crown, beautiful and golden,
> on her immortal head
> and flowers of copper and precious gold
> in the pierced lobes of her ears.

The heavenly Venus arising from the sea has inspired hundreds of poets and artists through the ages, but it is the earthly Aphrodite who, through rapture, magic and desire, has held sway over men's lives. In the *Danaid* of Aeschylus she proudly extols her power:

> The holy heaven is full of desire to mate with the earth, and desire seizes the earth to find a mate; rain falls from the amorous heaven and impregnates the earth; and the earth brings forth for men the fodder of flocks and herds and the gifts of Demeter; and from the same moistening marriage-rite the fruit of trees is ripened. Of these things I am the cause.

Aphrodite embodies sexuality free of ambivalence, anxieties and self-consciousness, a sexuality so natural and quintessential to her that no myth deals with her virginity or its loss. She makes love to her young lover, Anchises, under the mid-day sun. She is the only goddess who glories in her nakedness, the only one to be portrayed nude in sculptures. At the same time, she is the goddess of all the arts that enhance beauty and love-making – of perfumes and incense, love-charms and potions, the use of oils and cosmetics and all the lore of aphrodisiac drinks and foods. She is the goddess of the cosmetics industry, the goddess of courtesans and the goddess of the courtesan in all women.

In our century Freud enthroned the instinct which the earthly Aphrodite embodies as the source of *all* instinct. His neglect of the other Aphrodite, the Uranian, the embodiment of the soul's desire, reflects the neglect in our own lives of an instinct less tangible but no less compelling. Each archetype, each god and goddess, has a dark side, but in Aphrodite magic brightness merges into swampy darkness. We have Botticelli's *Birth of Venus* and we have venereal diseases. We have Socrates' heavenly Aphrodite and we have neuroses, power-games, treacheries, all in the name of love. In Greece she was 'golden', 'glowing' Aphrodite, but she was also known as 'the dark one', 'the killer of men', 'the unholy'. She was closely connected with the Minoan 'goddess of wild things' and the Oriental goddess Ishtar, whose rites at Babylon, Byblos and Bambyce were notorious for their temple prostitution. Even in Corinth the priestesses at Aphrodite's temple were prostitutes or, as Pindar called them, 'daughters of persuasion'.

D.H.Lawrence called her the goddess of destruction: 'her white cold fire consumes and does not create'. And Marsilio Ficino's harangue against the goddess in Renaissance Florence is the classic attack of man's reason against a power that overwhelms it: 'Only Venus comes on openly as your friend, and is secretly your enemy. You should be attacking her if you are going to be attacking any of the gods. . . . She promises you her deadly pleasures and promises more than she ever delivers. . . .' Circe, Calypso, Cleopatra – they all embody Aphrodite the enchantress, the snare-knitter, the force men most fear and to which, at the same time, they are most irresistibly drawn. Those who try hardest to resist, those who imagine themselves immune to her power, are the ones on whom the goddess' wrath descends most vigorously: 'Do not imagine you can abdicate', W.H.Auden's Venus warns. 'Before you reach the frontier you are caught.'

The myths of Aphrodite are full of retaliations against those who forget her. She punished Daphnis, a Sicilian shepherd who won the hearts of nymphs and muses but insisted that love had no power over him; she caused the women of Lemnos, who neglected her, to exude a foul odour which repelled their husbands; and she destroyed Hippolytus. In her opening speech in Euripides' *Hippolytus* she explains why:

Great is my power and wide my fame among mortals and also in heaven. All men that look upon the light of the sun, all that dwell between the Euxine Sea and the boundaries of Atlas are under my sway: I bless those that respect my power, and disappoint those who are not humble towards me. Yes, even the family of gods have this trait: they are pleased when people respect them. I shall demonstrate the truth of this forthwith. Theseus' son Hippolytus, born of the Amazon and brought up by temperate Pittheus, is the only inhabitant of this land of Troezen who declares that I am the very vilest of divinities. He spurns love and will have nothing to do with sex. . . . It is his sinful neglect of *me* for which I shall punish Hippolytus this very day.

By Aphrodite's scheming, Phaedra, Theseus' wife, is smitten with a fearful love for her stepson. 'Moaning, and distraught with the pricks of love, love undeclared,' she is dying. Aphrodite's revenge is to reveal Phaedra's passion to her husband: Hippolytus is killed by his father's curses when a sea-monster rises from the water, frightens his horses and dashes his chariot to pieces.

Hippolytus is dead, but he is still moving among us in the men and women fighting against the lure of passion. Will-power, though, is a very insignificant force to pit against Aphrodite. To resist her is as futile as resisting life. 'Upon the yielding spirit', Euripides tells us, 'she comes gently, but to the proud and the fanatic heart she is a torturer with the brand of shame.'

The goddess herself is not immune from the wounds she inflicts and the passions she inspires. She is the longing she causes as well as the cause of longing. The myth of her love for Adonis, the beautiful youth born from the riven bark of the myrrh tree, has inspired some of the most moving and sensual poetry in Western literature. 'Thrice fairer than myself,' she calls him in Shakespeare's *Venus and Adonis*.

> 'Here come and sit, where never serpent hisses
> And being set, I'll smother thee with kisses.
>
> And yet not cloy thy lips with loathed satiety,
> But rather famish them amid their plenty,
> Making them red and pale with fresh variety –
> Ten kisses short as one, one long as twenty.' . . .
>
> She's Love, she loves, and yet she is not lov'd. . . .
>
> She red and hot as coals of glowing fire,
> He red for shame, but frosty in desire. . . .
>
> Being red, she loves him best; and being white,
> Her best is bettered with a more delight.
>
> Look how he can, she cannot choose but love. . . .

In the myth, Aphrodite and Persephone fought for Adonis' love. Their dispute was brought before Zeus, who decided that he should spend one third of the year with Persephone in the Underworld, one third with Aphrodite and one third by himself. When he was with Aphrodite, her life revolved around him: she sought only to please him (she is, after all, the goddess of the courtesans). He loved to hunt, so she would leave the swan-drawn chariot in which she used to glide through the air and trek through rough woodland to be with him at the chase. One day, when she was not with him, a boar gored him with its great tusks. His blood ran down, red anemones sprang up from the ground, and the goddess of love mourned and wept.

> With one sharp-taken breath,
> By sunlit branches and unshaken flower,
> The immortal limbs flashed to the human lover,
> And the immortal eyes to look on death.

Loss and death, unrequited love and abandonment, are all part of Aphrodite's realm. Indeed, only by these dark shadows does her golden brilliance become a complete creation, smiling its immortal smile as well as looking on death with immortal eyes. Permanence is of Hera's world, not Aphrodite's. What belongs to her is a deep acceptance that passionate love does not last forever; and an equally deep acceptance that man is made to love.

> Torches are made to light, jewels to wear,
> Dainties to taste, fresh beauty for the use,
> Herbs for their smell, and sappy plants to bear;
> Things growing to themselves are growth's abuse:
> Seeds spring from seeds, and beauty breedeth beauty;
> Thou wast begot; to get it is thy duty.

Aphrodite's essence is transformation through the power of beauty and love – the power that is responsible for all the metamorphoses that Ovid wrote about. Even Pygmalion, the legendary king of Cyprus, could only bring his ivory statue of the ideal woman to life by falling in love with it. 'Pygmalion gazed in wonder', Ovid tells us, 'and in his heart there rose a passionate love for this image of human form.' At the festival of Venus he made his offerings to the goddess and prayed to her.

> When Pygmalion returned home, he made straight for the statue of the girl he loved, leaned over the couch, and kissed her. She seemed warm: he laid his lips on hers again, and touched her breast with his hands – at his touch the ivory lost its hardness, and grew soft: his fingers made an imprint on the yielding

LEFT Terracotta head of Aphrodite, *c.* 300 BC. 'She who awakens a yearning in the gods, she who subdues the race of mortal men. . . .'

Homeric Hymn to Aphrodite

PAGE 86 Eros, Roman copy of a Greek original of the 5th century BC. Aphrodite's son stands in Greek religion for the principle of intercourse between the human and the divine. 'Eros embraces in his essence the phallic, the psychic and the spiritual, and even points beyond the life of the individual being.'

KARL KERÉNYI

PAGE 87 Roman statue of Aphrodite.

'. . . Yet, whatso'er of good,
Of crime, of pride, of passion, or
  of grace
In woman is, thou, woman, hast
  in sum.
Earth's archetypal Eve. All
  Womanhood.'

WILFRID SCAWEN BLUNT

surface, just as wax of Hymettus melts in the sun and, worked by men's fingers, is fashioned into many different shapes, and made fit for use by being used. The lover stood, amazed, afraid of being mistaken, his joy tempered with doubt, and again and again stroked the object of his prayers. It was indeed a human body! The veins throbbed as he pressed them with his thumb. Then Pygmalion was eloquent in his thanks to Venus. At long last, he pressed lips upon living lips, and the girl felt the kisses he gave her, and blushed. Timidly raising her eyes, she saw her lover and the light of day together.

The power that transforms is the same power that brings destruction and dissolution, the almighty desire that forgets the whole world for the sake of the beloved. It tears asunder all established structures, family ties and bonds of duty. But we can either drown in it or be released through it into a life lived more intensely, more truthfully, more consciously. In the *Phaedrus*, Socrates talks of 'divine madness' as a much higher form of being than 'man-made sanity'. He distinguishes four types of divine madness and ascribes them to four gods: 'the inspiration of the prophet to Apollo, that of the mystic to Dionysos, that of the poet to the Muses, and a fourth type which we declared to be the highest, the madness of the lover, to Aphrodite and Eros'.

It is the divine madness that removes the vagueness and dullness of habitual perceptions, that brings the sublime within the ken of earthly mortals. In the same way that all matter at a certain degree of heat becomes luminous, all men have experienced moments in their lives when they have felt the exaltation of love and beauty, the power of Aphrodite. Her power, the myths tell us, can either lead us to transformation or be dissipated, so that what was for a moment luminous becomes again opaque.

'If the all too obvious and the overly straight sprouts of Truth and Goodness have been crushed, cut down, or not permitted to grow, then perhaps the whimsical, unpredictable and ever-surprising shoots of Beauty will force their way through and soar up to that very spot, thereby fulfilling the task of all three.' This was part of Alexander Solzhenitsyn's Nobel Prize acceptance speech. But it could also have been a hymn to the two Aphrodites delivered for all time.

ABOVE Aphrodite reclining in the lap of her mother Dione, from the east pediment of the Parthenon, *c.* 437–432 BC.
'. . . And after strain
Relax in your darling's arms like a stone,
Remembering everything you can confess,
Making the most of firelight, of hours of fuss. . . .'

W. H. AUDEN

PAGE 90 Aphrodite emerging from the sea on the central panel of the Ludovisi Throne, *c.* 460 BC.
'In the blessed rose light of dawn, look how I rise, my arms held high. The sea's godlike calm bids me to ascend into blue air.
Nymphs of the breeze, hurry; Cymothoe, Glauce, come grip me under my arms. I did not think I'd find myself so suddenly caught up in the sun's embrace.' ANGELOS SIKELIANOS

RIGHT Aphrodite emerging from the sea, Roman copy of a Greek original of the 4th century BC or later. 'Embracing her, it is all the riches of life that the lover would possess.'

SIMONE DE BEAUVOIR

PAGE 91 Flute player on a side panel of the Ludovisi Throne, *c.* 460 BC.

PAGE 92 Relief of Zeus, 1st century AD. 'The eye of Zeus, seeing all and understanding all. . . .' HESIOD

PAGE 93 Relief of Demeter, holding wheat and poppy pods, 1st century AD.

DIONYSOS

PAGE 94 Dionysos riding a
panther, pebble mosaic from the
House of the Lion Hunt at Pella,
Macedonia, *c.* 300 BC. 'The
panther leaps as gracefully as a
Bacchant, and this is the reason
the god loves him so.'

PHILOSTRATUS

PAGE 95 Dionysos and Ariadne,
the woman whom the god of
women chooses and to whom he
remains eternally faithful, on the
bronze vessel of Derveni,
c. 330 BC.

LEFT Mosaic head of Dionysos
from a Roman villa at Corinth.
'Pour, Bacchus! the
    remembering wine;
Retrieve the loss of me and
    mine!
Vine for vine be antidote,
And the grape requite the lote!
Haste to cure the old despair, –
Reason in Nature's lotus
    drenched,
The memory of ages quenched.'

RALPH WALDO EMERSON

WE ARE AN APOLLONIAN PEOPLE living in an Apollonian civilization. Or so
we think until Dionysos rises from the depths and tears the Apollonian order
asunder. Dionysos, or Bacchus as he was known among both the Greeks and
the Romans, is the last god to enter Olympos. Hesiod only briefly alludes to
him, Homer does not admit him at all, and only Euripides, the most modern
of Greek poets, deals fully with him – in his last play. 'Too late you have
learned to know me', Euripides makes the god cry in the *Bacchae*, 'When the
knowledge was wanted, you had it not.' The myths of Dionysos are
dominated by an initial fierce resistance to the god, in the same way that we
refuse to recognize the wild forces in us until we are overwhelmed by their
power.

Our civilization has for centuries been in collision with the Dionysian
elements in man. As early as 186 BC the Roman Senate issued a proclamation
which suppressed all Bacchic societies throughout Italy as a conspiracy
against the state. And since then we have been banishing the Dionysian
forces in us to the depths of our psychic hinterland as a conspiracy against
reason and Apollonian control, against 'noble simplicity and quiet
grandeur'.

But as the chorus in the *Bacchae* proclaims, 'The gods are cunning: they lie
in wait a long march of time to trap the impious.' The Dionysian revolt
began in the nineteenth century with Nietzsche's *The Birth of Tragedy*. Freud
followed by throwing a glaring light on the darkness suppressed in our
unconscious. And Jung established the 'Dionysian' as a basic structure of our
psyche. What had been regarded as inferior, hysterical, unbridled and
dangerous aspects of life, to be dissected and tamed, began to be seen as vital
parts of ourselves, to be brought into consciousness. The god's myths and
modern history and psychology tell the same story: however hard we

oppose, suppress or resist him, Dionysos is invincible.

'The Bull, the underground Dionysian power, has been unleashed', warned Kazantzakis in *The Odyssey*, echoing the wise Tiresias' warning to the king of Thebes: 'This new divinity whom you ridicule – words cannot describe how great will be his power throughout Hellas. . . . Listen to *me*. . . . Do not presume that mere power has influence with men. Do not be wise in your diseased imagination. Welcome the god to the land, pour libations, wreathe your head, revel.'

A late *Homeric Hymn* in honour of the god tells a story that is a beautiful symbol both of the god's mystery and of his destructiveness when we attempt to imprison and suppress him.

What I remember now is Dionysos, son of glorious Semele, how he appeared by the sand of an empty sea, how it was far out, on a promontory, how he was like a young man, an adolescent. His dark hair was beautiful, it blew all around him, and over his shoulders, the strong shoulders, he held a purple cloak. Suddenly, pirates appeared, Tyrrhenians, they came on the wine sea sturdily in their ship and they came fast. A wicked fate drove them on. They saw him, they nodded to each other, they leaped out and grabbed him, they pulled him into their boat jumping for joy! They thought he was the son of one of Zeus' favourite kings; they wanted to tie him up hard. The ropes wouldn't hold. Willow ropes, they fell right off him, off arms and legs. He smiled at them, motionless, in his dark eyes.

The helmsman saw this, he immediately cried out, he screamed out to his men: 'You fools! What powerful god is this whom you've seized, whom you've tied up? Not even our ship, sturdy as it is, not even our ship can carry him. . . . Don't tie his hands or he'll be angry, he'll draw terrible winds to us, he'll bring us a big storm!' That's what he said. The captain, however, in a bitter voice, roared back: 'You fool, look at the wind! Grab the rope, draw the sail. We men will take care of him. . . .'

He said this, then he fixed the mast and the sail of the ship. And a wind began to blow into the sail. And then they stretched the rigging. Suddenly, wonderful things appeared to them. First of all, wine broke out, babbling, bubbling over their speedy black ship, it was sweet, it was fragrant, its odour was divine. Every sailor who saw it was terrified. Suddenly, a vine sprang up, on each side, to the very top of the sail. And grapes, all over, clung to it. And a dark ivy coiled the mast, it blossomed with flowers and yielded pleasing fruit. Suddenly, all the oar-locks became garlands. When they saw this they cried to the helmsman then and there to steer their ship to land. But the god became a lion, an awful lion high up on the ship, and he roared at them terribly. And then, in their midst, he put a bear, a bear with a furry neck, and it made gestures. It threatened, and the lion, on the high deck, scowled down. Everybody fled to the stern, they panicked, they ran to the helmsman, because

Marble relief of Dionysos, accompanied by a panther, 2nd century A D.

the head of the helmsman was cool. But the lion, suddenly, leaped up, it seized the captain! They all wanted to escape such a doom when they saw it. They all jumped ship into the sea, they jumped into the divine sea. They became dolphins. As for the helmsman, he was saved: the god pitied him, he made him very rich, and told him this: 'Courage, divine Hecator, I like you. I am Dionysos the ear-splitter. My mother, Cadmaean Semele, had me when she slept with Zeus.'

The god who destroys those who try to hold him in bondage is also the benevolent god who rewards with life and abundance those who recognize his divinity and his power. The miracles on the pirates' ship are similar to the miracles accompanying the god's epiphany at his festivals and proclaiming the god's presence in his myths. Wine streams forth, vines with swelling grapes appear, ivy grows, honey trickles down, water or milk gushes forth. The mystery which calls forth nourishing or intoxicating streams is the same mystery which splits rocks, bursts chains asunder and causes walls to crumble. Dionysos is the god of ecstasy, dance and song; he is also Lysios, 'the loosener', 'the liberator'. He brings plasticity and flexibility into what is rigid and hard; he frees us from old bondages; he dissolves old claims; he lifts the age-old barriers which conceal the invisible and the infinite. And the infinite vitality that had been locked away wells up from the depths like the milk, honey and wine that spurt forth from the earth.

> The world man knows, the world in which he has settled himself so securely and smugly – that world is no more. The turbulence which accompanied the arrival of Dionysos has swept it away. Everything has been transformed. But it has not been transformed into a charming fairy story or into an ingenuous child's paradise. The primeval world has stepped into the foreground, the depths of reality have been opened, the elemental forms of everything that is creative, everything that is destructive, have arisen, bringing with them infinite rapture and infinite terror. The innocent picture of a well-ordered routine world has been shattered by their coming, and they bring with them no illusions or fantasies, but truth.

It is a truth that brings joy, liberation, renewal, but also madness.

The double nature of the god was symbolized in the double nature of wine which was the gift the god of intoxicated delight gave to men. Countless myths tell of the power, the magic of wine which conquered 'even the Centaurs'. Yet in the same drink which has in it 'the power to free, to comfort and to bring bliss, there slumbers also the madness of the god of horror'. In the *Laws*, Plato, recognizing the double nature of wine, seeks to limit its dangers by prescribing its use according to age:

> In the first place, we shall absolutely prohibit the taste of wine to boys under

RIGHT The theatre of Dionysos in Athens was rebuilt in stone *c.*342–326 BC to replace the earlier wooden one where the plays of Aeschylus, Sophocles, Euripides and Aristophanes were first performed.

PAGE 102 Dionysos as a young man, Roman copy of a Greek original of the 4th century BC. 'The Praise of Bacchus then the sweet Musician sung, Of Bacchus ever Fair, and ever Young. . . .' DRYDEN

PAGE 103 Drunken Dionysos supported by a young satyr, from the lid of a bronze vessel, *c.*300 BC. Wine in Bacchic religion was a sacrament used to produce a state of *ekstasis* (standing outside oneself) and *enthusiasmos* (possession by the god).

Head of Dionysos on a silver coin of Naxos, 430–420 BC. It is a greater life, beyond conventions, inertia and fear, that Dionysos embodies – life in the round, forever coming into being, forever renewing itself, forever dying and being reborn.

eighteen. We shall tell them they must have too much concern for the passionate temperament of youth to feed the fire of body or soul with a further current of fire before they address themselves to the labours of life. In the next, while we permit a moderate use of wine to men under thirty, we shall absolutely forbid carousing and free potations. But when a man is verging on the forties, we shall tell him, after he has finished banqueting at the general table, to invoke the gods, and more particularly to ask the presence of Dionysos in the sacrament and pastime of advancing years – I mean the wine cup – which he bestowed on us for a comfortable medicine against the dryness of old age, that we might renew our youth, and our harsher mood be melted to softness by forgetfulness of our heaviness, as iron is melted in the furnace, and so made more tractable. To begin with, in that mood, any man would be ready, would he not, to render his song – or, as we have so often called it, his spell – with more spirit and less bashfulness.

Song and dance, 'with more spirit and less bashfulness', were such primary expressions of Dionysian emotion that he is said to have sung and danced already as a baby in his mother's womb. The reed-pipe, the drums and the cymbals are all instruments of the god, accompanying the dance of his Maenads. 'He who knows the power of the dance dwells in God', Jelaluddin Rumi, a founder of the Dervishes, has said, and Dionysian dancing springs from the same source as the dancing of the Whirling Dervishes and the Jewish Hasidim, the Siberian Shaman and Shiva the Cosmic Dancer. In its highest expression, the aim of the dance is not to induce a trance, it is not ecstasy and release, but a mystic communion with the divine. 'When your body is spinning', the Dervishes say, 'there is a completely still point in the

Silenus, Dionysos' elderly and usually drunken companion, who had the ears and tail of a horse, on the reverse of the coin shown opposite.

centre. When you dance, all the stars, and the planets, and the endless universes dance around that still point. The heavens respond; and invisible kingdoms join in the dance.'

Music and dance come from the depths of life, and from the same elemental depths come also inspired art and prophecy. Here Dionysos is the enemy of rigid dignity and self-control, and man is on the threshold of madness. Plato says in *Ion*:

> As the worshipping Corybantes are not in their senses when they dance, so the lyric poets are not in their senses when they make these lovely lyric poems. No, when once they launch into harmony and rhythm, they are seized with the Bacchic transport, and are possessed – as the bacchants, when possessed, draw milk and honey from the rivers, but not when in their senses. . . . A poet is a light and winged thing, and holy, and never able to compose until he has become inspired, and is beside himself, and reason is no longer in him. So long as he has this in his possession, no man is able to make poetry or to chant in prophecy. . . . For not by art do they utter these, but by power divine. . . . It is not they who utter these precious revelations while their mind is not within them, but the god himself who speaks, and through them becomes articulate to us.

Dionysos embodies this madness of the supreme moment of creation, of the enchanted moment when man is flung out of his routine world, his settled thoughts and feelings, his ordered existence, and dives into the cosmic depths in which the forces of life dwell. 'This madness which is called Dionysos is no sickness, but a companion of life at its healthiest.'

In ancient Greece, it was the women whose lives were traditionally most confined who became the god's most enthusiastic worshippers. The god 'pricks them to leave their looms and shuttles'. Again and again in the god's myths we come across Argive women, Rhodian women, Athenian women, ripped loose from the humdrum, orderly activities of their domestic lives and, intoxicated by the god, being transformed into enraptured, manic dancers in the wilderness of the mountains.

> They gird themselves with snakes and give suck to fawns and wolf cubs as if they were infants at the breast. Fire does not burn them. No weapon of iron can wound them, and the snakes harmlessly lick up the sweat from their heated cheeks. Fierce bulls fall to the ground, victims to numberless, tearing, female hands, and sturdy trees are torn up by the roots with their combined effort.

Once again, we are confronted with the god's double nature: the bringer of liberation, ecstasy, inspiration and the most blessed deliverance is also the bringer of madness, violence, wildness, terror. He is known as 'the roarer', 'the loud-shouter', 'the ear-splitter', but he is just as powerfully revealed in the fathomless silence as in the pandemonium that he stirs up. He appears as a bull, a bear, a lion, a panther, but he also transforms himself into a young girl, a tree, flowing water. The numinous feeling that he inspires shatters all order and composure and can lead either to the ecstatic experience of the divine or to hysteria and bloodthirsty destructiveness.

The outcome, the god's myths tell us, depends on the response of the established consciousness. In the *Bacchae*, the god is described as 'serene and dignified' until the blind rationalism of Pentheus, the king of Thebes, brings about the tragedy's manic destruction. 'Take to arms', is the king's response, but spears and armour are powerless against the elemental forces which Pentheus chokes off and resists and which Dionysos embodies and celebrates. The paradox baffles but cannot be evaded: enlightenment and destruction, life and death, are indissolubly linked.

The instinctual life-force that Dionysos represents is in perpetual opposition to all that is dead and petrified in us but remains bolstered by habit, inertia and fear. And the god will use every means to tame the forces that resist life – including the whip of madness, horror and destruction. Dionysos was the god of the theatre, and horror, whether in his myths or on stage, was used to evoke the emotional, instinctual levels of man's being – to move the soul. Emotions and thoughts previously pent up were released, and under the god's sway 'the unutterable could be spoken and the unthinkable could be staged'. What had been submerged could come to the surface in all its splendour and all its darkness, and the primordial human needs for communion and participation could find fulfilment.

Aristotle described the catharsis that takes place through tragedy as the purification and purging of the emotions of the spectator through his experience of pity and terror. And the choral songs (dithyrambs) and dark rites performed as part of the god's worship are the ritual origins of Greek and therefore of all Western tragedy.

The most powerful symbol of the god and his two-fold nature was the mask worn by the actors. The mask has since primitive times been a sacred object of awe. The wearer of the mask is himself – and yet he is not. He evokes the mystery of a dual reality where what we see is not what is, and what is transcends what we see. It is the spirit of Dionysos that confronts man through the penetrating eyes of the mask, shattering all the mind's certainties.

> The final secrets of existence and non-existence transfix mankind with monstrous eyes. . . . Here there is nothing but encounter, from which there is no withdrawal. . . . Because it is the god's nature to appear suddenly and with overwhelming might before mankind, the mask serves as his symbol and his incarnation in cult. The mask has no reverse side. 'Spirits have no backs', people say. It has nothing which might transcend the mighty moment of confrontation. It is the symbol and the manifestation of that which is simultaneously there and not there: that which is excruciatingly near, that which is completely absent – both in one reality.

It is a fitting image for the god of the here and now, of overwhelming immediacy, who is at the same time the god of inexpressible distance, the god of eternity – the god who holds life and death together. As the only Olympian god to be born of a mortal mother, Dionysos is from the beginning more closely associated with death than any other god except Hades. His mother's death by the fire of Zeus' lightning-bolts while he was still in her womb and his second birth from the body of Zeus himself strengthen his connection to the mystery of life and death cemented together in an eternal unity. It is a connection which persists in all his myths as he thrusts men into a new life, overflowing with rapture and vitality – a life into which they can only be born by dying to their past and to everything they cling to for security, an inexhaustible life born of pain and death.

Nowhere do we see this more clearly and more movingly than in the myth of Dionysos and Ariadne, the woman whom the god of women chooses and to whom he remains eternally faithful – the only faithful husband among the amorous gods. But before Dionysos' beloved can be fully united with him in inexhaustible life and immortality, she must go through deep suffering and, in some versions of the myth, even death. In

Monteverdi's opera *Arianna*, Arianna's Lament so caught the public's imagination that it became overnight the most popular piece of music of the moment. The Cretan princess, daughter of King Minos, wakes on a lonely beach on Naxos to discover that Theseus, the man whose life she has saved, has abandoned her.

Theseus had arrived in Crete as part of the Athenian tribute of seven men and seven women who were sent to Crete every nine years to be sacrificed to the Minotaur – the terrible monster that was half-bull and half-man. Theseus could only be saved and be free to return to Athens if he entered the Labyrinth and slew the Minotaur. All who had gone before him had perished, but Theseus, guided by the thread Ariadne had given him, was able to make his way into the Labyrinth and come out of it alive and victorious. He left Crete, taking Ariadne with him, only to desert her on the first island where their ship put anchor for the night. He abandons her because, as Homer implies, she has to be abandoned. Her desertion by Theseus, by the mortal part of herself, is the necessary prelude to her relationship with Dionysos, who embodies the transcendent in her. 'At times we are pulled to an involvement with a human other as an escape from a connection with the transcendent, a connection with a prior claim on us that is somehow too much. We flee to the heroic mortal lover, escaping from the deeper experience. . . . At the moments when what Dionysos represents is more than we feel we can handle or stay in touch with, we turn our backs on it.' The prior claim of Dionysos, of the divine, is expressed in the myth in concrete terms: Ariadne was already Dionysos' beloved before she betrayed him for Theseus.

'I will never love again, and therefore in some sense I will never live again', cries the deserted Ariadne in Richard Strauss' opera. At the moment of her deepest despair, Dionysos is heard singing off-stage. She hails him as the longed-for messenger of death. But when he appears before her, she recognizes in him her true lover for whom, transformed through her pain, she is now ready. The opera ends with a ravishing love duet; the myth ends with Ariadne's ascent to heaven in the god's chariot. Her suffering and lamentation are transformed into bliss in the god's arms.

Ariadne's thread is the symbolic counterpart of Dionysos' mask: it connects this world with the other, the outer with the inner, mortality with eternity. Ariadne's cult on Naxos, with its festivals of joy and of sorrow, captures the spirit of the god: sorrow, suffering, terror, even death, are all in the service of a greater life, liberated from rationalist limitations and conventional imprisonments. It is this greater life that Dionysos embodies – life in the round, forever coming into being, forever renewing itself, forever dying and being reborn.

ABOVE Reclining Dionysos from the east pediment of the Parthenon, *c.* 437–432 BC.

PAGE 110 Roman mosaic of vine growing.
'Wine expands, unites, and says Yes: it brings the votary from the chill periphery of things to the radiant core: it makes him for the moment one with truth.' WILLIAM JAMES

PAGE 111 The sanctuary of Dionysos at Ikaria (modern Dionisos) in Attica where Dionysos was entertained by the farmer Ikarios. In return for his hospitality the god taught him the art of making wine.

PAGE 112 Dancing girl on a plaque found in the theatre of Dionysos in Athens, Roman copy of a Greek original of 350–300 BC. 'I have instituted my dances and my mysteries, that my godhead might be manifest to mortals. . . I have filled Thebes with the cries of exultant women; I have fitted the fawn-skin to their bodies and have put into their hands the militant thyrsus, entwined with ivy. . . .' EURIPIDES, *Bacchae*

PAGE 113 The theatre at Side in Turkey, 2nd century AD. 'The theatre of mythology – the stage, the players, and the audience – is the human being.' KARL KERÉNYI

ZEUS

ZEUS, THE 'ALL-SEEING' AND 'ALL-HIGH', lord of air and sky, is the personification of the principle of order and consciousness that illuminates all. His very name comes from the Indo-European root *dyu*, 'to shine'. But before he can establish his kingdom of light and luminous justice, he has to face two terrible ordeals. He has to overcome his devouring father, Cronos, and he has to defeat the Titans, the huge, monstrous representatives of the great Earth Mother, Gaia. The character of Zeus as the politician among the gods is immediately established by the means he uses to gain supremacy. Against the brute force of the Titans he deploys an uncanny instinct for strategy and for consolidating his power by key alliances with the older divinities. He frees the Cyclopes and the Hundred-armed Giants from the dungeon in the bowels of the earth where they were kept imprisoned, feeds them nectar and ambrosia and, having restored their fighting spirit, Hesiod tells us, he chooses the moment to address them:

> You fine sons of Earth and Sky, listen while I tell you what is in my mind. For a long time now there has been warfare every day between the Titan generation of gods and the children of Cronos to decide which shall be the victors and have the supreme power. Your duty is to employ the great strength of your invincible arms in the stress of battle on our side against the Titans; remember that we have been your good friends, and that you are indebted to our action for your release from the agony of imprisonment and for your return from the dark underworld to the light of day.

Since he carries, after all, the archetypal essence of the political strategist, both his timing and the words he chooses are impeccable and bring forth the precise response he intends: 'Son of Cronos, you are our master . . . we will join the bloody battle against the Titans and strengthen your side with

Marble head of Zeus, Roman copy of a Greek original of the 5th century BC.
'Hail, O Zeus, most glorious of the immortals, named by many names, forever all-powerful, leader of nature, you who govern the universe with laws; for it is proper that all mortals should call upon you. For from you we are born; of all mortal things that live and move upon the earth the only ones created in the god's image. So I will praise you, and always sing of your power. . . .'
CLEANTHES, *Hymn to Zeus*

unflagging energy and loyal hearts.' The new allies did not just bring Zeus unflagging energy and loyal hearts: they brought him the thunder and the lightning-bolts, the gifts from the Cyclopes that determined the battle.

Once victorious, Zeus establishes the new cosmic order – an order based not on brute strength but on intellectual surpremacy, and, above all, on alliances and matings both sacred and political. He allies himself with the depths, from which the Cyclopes bring him the lightning-bolts, instruments and emblems of his power; he mates with Themis, the old goddess of law, and brings forth Good Order, Justice and Peace; with Eurynome and produces the three Graces; with Mnemosyne and produces the nine Muses; with Leto and produces Artemis and Apollo.

His essence, in its most positive aspect, is creative proliferation, the light of consciousness that impregnates the latent powers of law, wisdom and beauty and actualizes them. Even the older powers that he defeats are not actually destroyed. Cronos is sent to rule over the 'Island of the Blessed' and the Titans are sent to Tartarus; the 'Island of the Blessed' may be 'at the end of the world' and Tartarus 'as far below the ground as the ground is below the sky', but they are still *within* the world over which Zeus rules. The new consciousness is secure enough to include the depths; in fact it is secure only so long as it rules over them but does not deny their existence. When the one god forgets the other gods, cries out Prometheus in Aeschylus' *Prometheus Bound*, he will die. He will die because he will have negated the powers that feed and strengthen the supremacy of consciousness that he represents.

Theos (god) was used almost interchangeably with Zeus by the Greeks. In his essential ability to integrate all powers in him, Zeus comes closest to the monotheistic ideal – the one in whom the many are reconciled, the highest single principle in which the tension of opposites is resolved. When participants in the Orphic mysteries went on to exalt the supreme god that permeates all, they called him Zeus:

> Zeus is the first, Zeus is the last, the god with the dazzling lightning. Zeus is the head, Zeus is the middle, of Zeus all things have their end. Zeus is the foundation of the earth and of the starry sky. Zeus is male, Zeus is an immortal woman. Zeus is the breath of all things, Zeus is the sweep of unwearying flame. Zeus is the roots of the sea, Zeus is the sun and moon. Zeus is the King, Zeus is the beginner of all things, the god with the dazzling lightning. For he has hidden all things within himself, and brought them forth again, into the joyful light, from his sacred heart, working marvels.

Orpheus and his followers worshipped Zeus as 'the breath of all things'; the people sacrificed to him as 'the helper of men', 'the warder-off of evil', 'the god that dispenses all good things', 'the god of the suppliant, the healer

Corinthian columns of the temple of Zeus in Athens. 'Zeus is the air, Zeus the earth, and Zeus the sky, Zeus everything, and all that is more than these.'
AESCHYLUS

Mt Dicte, in Crete, where Zeus was
born and raised. 'The portion of
Zeus is the broad heaven, in
brightness and in cloud alike.'
HOMER, *Iliad*

of guilt'; Hesiod praised him as the guardian of law and morals; the Stoics identified him with the principles of reason and fire that animate the universe; Aeschylus celebrated him as the god of gods, just and omnipotent. But the aspect of Zeus that has fascinated poets through the ages is Zeus the lover. The Catalogue Aria in Mozart's *Don Giovanni* could have been written for him. He mated with goddesses and nymphs, princesses and mortal women; he changed into a bull to ravish Europa as she was picking flowers by the seashore; into a shower of gold to penetrate Danaë; into a swan to couple with Leda; into an eagle to catch Asteria who had turned herself into a quail; into Amphitryon to make love to his wife Alcmena.

> Ageless, lusty, he twists into bull, ram, serpent,
> Swan, gold rain; a hundred wily disguises
> To catch girl, nymph or goddess; begets tall heroes,
> Monsters, deities, gets Troy's fall and the long history
> Of many a wandering after, pestilence, death in exile,
> Founding of hearths and cities. All that scribe or sculptor
> Chronicle is no more than fruit of his hot embraces
> With how many surprised recumbent breasts and haunches.
> Look, they say, from his play is law begotten,
> Peace between tribe and tribe, converse of merchants,
> Trust, the squared stone, the ordered grave procession.
> Maybe it is so.
> All he knew was the law that stiffened his member
> Seeing a girl's soft hair curled down on her shoulders.
> A tale more likely.
>
> GRAHAM HOUGH

> A sudden blow: the great wings beating still
> Above the staggering girl, her thighs caressed
> By the dark webs, her nape caught in his bill,
> He holds her helpless breast upon his breast.
>
> How can those terrified vague fingers push
> The feathered glory from her loosening thighs?
> And how can body, laid in that white rush,
> But feel the strange heart beating where it lies?
>
> A shudder in the loins engenders there
> The broken wall, the burning roof and tower
> And Agamemnon dead.
>   Being so caught up,
> So mastered by the brute blood of the air,
> Did she put on his knowledge with his power
> Before the indifferent beak could let her drop?
>
> W. B. YEATS

RIGHT 'Rugged Olympos', the home of the gods. 'Father . . . do not stop ascending in front of us, but climb always with slow even wings the heavens of our Thought, eternal Daedalus, Dawnstar of the Beyond.'
ANGELOS SIKELIANOS

PAGE 122 Zeus' temple at Nemea, 4th century BC.

PAGE 123 'Now I am also a thing of the world in your hands, the tiniest under this sky . . . .
What a wonderful building, moving inside itself, held up by itself,
forming figures, giant wings, canyons,
and high mountains, before the first star. . . .'
RAINER MARIA RILKE

PAGE 124 Hera's temple at Paestum in southern Italy, begun in the 6th century BC. Paestum was founded in the 7th century BC by Greek settlers, and this is the earliest of the three temples that they built.

PAGE 125 Zeus' temple in Athens, 6th century BC– 2nd century AD. 'It is the only temple on earth of a size adequate to the greatness of the god.'   LIVY

Only one woman, Semele, the daughter of the founder of Thebes, begged her lover to reveal himself in his full splendour and majesty. Reluctantly he did, and the fire of his divine radiance destroyed her. In a poem by the nineteenth-century English poet Coventry Patmore, Semele dies fulfilled: at least she has had a clear vision of the divine. In the myth, just before she dies, Zeus snatches from her womb the child she is bearing, sews it into his thigh and gives birth himself to the god Dionysos.

It is in the nature of myth that it can be experienced and understood on many different levels, but the stories of Zeus the lover are so imaginative, so rich, so colourful, at the first, most accessible level, that we can easily get lost in their poetry and sensuality. And the sexual imagery is so vivid and compelling that we can, just as easily, succumb to the temptation of analysing them, as many have done, in terms of Zeus' promiscuity, his flagrant display of sexual potency or his underlying sexual insecurity.

When we turn again to Zeus' essence as the light of consciousness, we see in his sexual couplings with earthly women a beautiful metaphor for the impregnation of matter by spirit. The divine descends on earth and the result is *always* a new birth. Zeus' love-making is never sterile, and the fruit of the divine and human embrace is invariably a higher order of being – a god or a hero. There may be pain in the process, but then there seldom is birth of consciousness without pain.

It is Zeus' marriage to Hera, *the* marriage on Olympos, that is, in fact, the least fruitful of his unions. Hera is his sister as well as his wife, and so doubly his equal and in no need of his fertilizing energy, either for offspring (Hephaistos, Typhon and Ares are all Hera's fatherless sons) or for consciousness.

In one of the most beautiful and powerful passages in the *Iliad*, in a striking reversal of the pattern associated with Zeus, it is Hera who initiates their love-making and seduces him on the highest peak of Mt Ida as he is busily watching the progress of events on the battlefield of Troy.

> So speaking, the son of Cronos caught his wife in his arms.
> There underneath them the divine earth broke into young,
> fresh grass, and into dewy clover, crocus and hyacinth so
> thick and soft it held the hard ground deep away from them.
> There they lay down together and drew about them a golden
> wonderful cloud, and from it the glimmering dew descended.

Hera in her positive aspect embodies the instinct for the deep mutuality of the 'sacred marriage'. She does not need Zeus to complete herself. What she needs is to be 'fully met, matched, mated', sexually, intellectually, spiritually. In Zeus' refusal to be deeply, sacredly, married to her we begin to

PAGE 126 Fallen column drums from Zeus' temple at Olympia. 'Stone, steel, dominions pass, Faith too, no wonder....'
A. E. HOUSMAN

PAGE 127 The sanctuary of Hera, patron goddess of the Argolid, near Argos.

LEFT 'The sun, the child of Hyperion, was descending into the golden bowl to cross the Ocean and reach the depths of the holy dark night....'
STESICHORUS

LEFT Roman statue of Castor, the son of Zeus and Leda, one of his mortal lovers. Zeus' love-making was never sterile and the fruit of the divine and human embrace was invariably a higher order of being – a god or a hero. Castor and his brother Polydeuces, 'the heavenly twins', were Argonauts and the special patrons of sailors.

PAGE 132 Zeus and Ganymede, 500–475 BC. Ganymede, Homer tells us, was the most beautiful of mortal men. Zeus carried him off to Olympos to be his cupbearer. Michelangelo, Correggio, Rubens and Rembrandt painted him; Marlowe and Tennyson immortalized him as Zeus' youthful lover; Xenophon and the allegorizers of the Middle Ages and the Renaissance extolled his intellect and his unsullied soul that made him the god's beloved.

PAGE 133 Ganymede and the eagle, 2nd century AD.
'Or else flush'd Ganymede, his rosy thigh
Half-buried in the eagle's down. . . .' TENNYSON

see the dark tones behind Zeus' brilliant figure.

The god who embodies the forces of expansion and growth seems incapable of the inner growth and expansion which come from the deep connection that marriage signifies in its real rather than its social sense. And this rigidity and aloofness spill over from the personal domain to the social and political one, in his aspect as the 'angry, retributive god' who metes out the harshest punishments for human transgressions, especially the transgressions of men guilty of hubris – the pride of attempting to overstep the measure of humanity. Bellerophon, who with the help of Athena and the winged horse Pegasus has defeated the Amazons, is hurled down by Zeus' thunderbolts when he tries to mount still higher on his flying horse and gain the luminous heights of heaven; Phaethon, Apollo's son, who takes the fiery chariot of the sun across the heavens, is hurled into the vast abyss by Zeus, despite Apollo's plea for his son's life; and Prometheus, who stole the divine fire from Olympos, is chained naked to a rock by Zeus, who sends a hungry vulture day after day, year after year, to tear at his liver.

The divine Zeus, who in his glory is the god who appears as light and brings light and consciousness to the humans, becomes in his darkness an enemy of the life-force, locked in his structures and laws, fearing and resisting change and any threat to the *status quo*. The planet Jupiter displays the same essential ambivalence. Traditionally known as the planet of expansion and wisdom, it can also act on the personality as dogmatism, stagnation and blind adherence to old habits and conventions. The force that expands and creates becomes the power that binds and restricts.

ABOVE Zeus' temple at Stratos, the ancient capital of Acarnania, 4th century BC. Zeus' sites are not those of the greatest drama. They seem to reflect the essence of the king of the gods: majestic dominion transcending conflict and struggle.

RIGHT The theatre at Dodona, *c.* 300 BC. The oracle of Zeus at Dodona was the oldest in Greece, and it is to the Zeus at Dodona that Achilles prays in the *Iliad*: 'High Zeus, lord of Dodona, Pelasgian, living afar off, brooding over wintry Dodona, your prophets about you living. . . . Hear me.'

LEFT Deidamia, bride of Pirithous, being abducted by the Centaur Eurytion, from the west pediment of the temple of Zeus at Olympia, *c.*460 BC.

ABOVE Lapith and Centaur fighting, metope from the south face of the Parthenon, *c.*448–442 BC. The Centaurs, half-horses, half-men, symbolize the essential duality of man. In fact in the whole of Greek mythology there is no firm line between virtue and sin, heroes and villains, perfect gods and imperfect men. The psychic forces the gods represent, negative and positive, are not isolated into neat compartments; there is a constant flow and connection among them.

ATHENA

THE MYTH OF ATHENA, ALL HYMNS TO HER, all references in Greek drama, begin with her beginning from the father:

> By the artifice of Hephaistos,
> at the stroke of the bronze-heeled axe Athena sprang
> from the height of her father's head with a strong cry.
> The sky shivered before her and earth our mother.
>
> PINDAR

> I'll start this singing with that grand goddess,
> Pallas Athena, bright-eyes, so shrewd,
> her heart inexorable, as virgin, redoubtable,
> protectress of cities, powerful,
> Tritogene, whom shrewd Zeus himself
> produced out of his sacred head.
>
> *Homeric Hymn to Athena*

> The man is the source of life – the one who mounts
> She, like a stranger for a stranger, keeps
> the shoot alive unless god hurts the roots
>
> I give you proof that all I say is true.
> The father can father forth without a mother.
> Here she stands, our living witness.
>
> Child sprung full-blown from Olympian Zeus,
> never bred in the darkness of the womb
> but such a stock no goddess could conceive!
>
> APOLLO IN AESCHYLUS' *Eumenides*

It is a beginning that the virgin goddess proudly acknowledges:

Bronze statue of Athena, mid 4th century BC.
'She threw round her shoulders the formidable tasselled aegis, which is beset at every point with Fear, and carries Strife and Force and the cold nightmare Pursuit within it, and also bears the ghastly image of a Gorgon's head, the grim and redoubtable emblem of aegis-bearing Zeus. On her head she put her golden helmet, with its four plates and double crest, adorned with fighting men of a hundred towns.' HOMER, *Iliad*

> No mother gave me birth.
> I honour the male, in all things but marriage.
> Yes, with all my heart I am my Father's child.
> <div align="right">ATHENA IN AESCHYLUS' <i>Eumenides</i></div>

She is not only her father's child, but the father's favourite, the only one who knows where the lightning-bolts are hidden, the only one who uses the *aegis*, Zeus' magically potent shield. In the ultimate Olympian trinity of Zeus-Athena-Apollo, Homer places Athena second, immediately after the king of the gods.

Athena's essence springs from this primary relationship with the father and the masculine order that he represents. She has absorbed aggression and transmuted it into a compelling strength that belongs to woman as much as to man. Athena's emergence, fully armed and independent, from Zeus' head, her total ease in the practical world of men whether on the battlefield or in the city, her inventive creativity, her involvement with law, justice and politics, all symbolize the great gift she can give modern woman: the realization that creation and action are as inherently natural to a woman as to a man. Athena frees women from the fear of trespassing into a masculine domain, the fear of throwing themselves into what Anaïs Nin called 'the aggressive act of creation, the guilt of creating. I did not want to rival man, to steal man's creation, his thunder.' Athena does not have to steal the lightning-bolts; she has complete access to them and freedom to use them.

She fully aligns herself with the masculine order, but she breathes into it soul, mercy, wisdom. She is, above all others, the goddess of civilization. 'Cities are the gift of Athena'; artisans, craftsmen and tradesmen celebrate her as their teacher and patroness; the male brotherhoods of the city worship her as their goddess. She is woman as inventress and woman as artisan. She invented the arts of pottery, of weaving, of measuring, and she was also the couturière of Olympos. When Hera wanted to lure her husband away from the action on the battlefield, she turned to Athena to make her robe, and when Zeus created the first woman, Pandora, to seduce mankind, he asked Athena to weave her dress.

In the *Statesman*, Plato uses Athena's weaving as a metaphor for the political process, and provides the bridge between Athena's nurturing of the arts that sustain the life of the community and her patronage of the art that binds the community together. James Hillman strikingly amplifies the metaphor:

> Inclusion of the excessive and abnormal by weaving it in is the art of political consciousness. Such weaving is not patching quilts, tacking boards, stitching leather, darning holes. It is not repairing. It is not collage. It is not bricolage,

haphazard, without inner necessity. Rather, Athena's art is the systematic plaiting of strands together; and as her own person is a combination of Reason and Necessity, her art of combination produces a whole fabric. All strands find place in and contribute. . . . The old Furies brought in, nothing left out, no extremities hanging over the edges: integration as ideal norm.

The art she draws on for her political weaving is the art of persuasion. Right words in the mouth of Athena become healing, restorative, moving the dark elements both within man and within the state into co-operation. In Aeschylus' *Eumenides*, she conceives the jury as a means of attaining an ideal of justice beyond primitive revenge. 'Persuasion guided my mouth', she explains when she wins the climactic argument with the Furies and saves Orestes' life.

Athena's use of the art of persuasion is most powerfully portrayed in her protection and guidance of her beloved heroes: of Herakles, Perseus, Jason, Achilles and, above all, Odysseus. 'I love them', she says in the *Eumenides*, 'as a gardener loves his plants, these upright men, this breed fought free of grief.' In the *Iliad*, as Achilles is about to draw his sword to slay Agamemnon who has announced his intention to take Achilles' concubine for himself, the goddess intervenes: 'Cease', she whispers. Athena is standing beside Achilles, personifying his own inner wisdom, whispering, yet clearly heard over the tumult of wilder passions. She represents both 'the nearness of the divine at the moment of severest trial' and the embodiment of the wise counsellor we all carry in us. 'She always stands beside me in all my tasks and always remembers me wherever I go,' says Odysseus, whose devotion to her is complete. For Odysseus, she is first among the immortals, the one who personifies his own clear-eyed sagacity and eloquence, sense of balance and shrewdness, his vision of homecoming in the midst of heroic adventures.

She guides Odysseus everywhere, except on his journey into the Underworld. Here Hermes takes over. Athena's domain is *this* world, and her reluctance to penetrate the mysteries of what lies below is the chink in the armour of the goddess of civilization. We shake the kaleidoscope and the goddess who 'outfaces the sun in brilliance' is seen as the goddess who denies her connection with the depths, with her own womanliness, with Gaia, the Goddess Earth, the Great Mother. Athena is the goddess of what W. H. Auden in his *Ode to Gaea* called 'this new culture of the air':

But why we should feel neglected on mountain drives,
unpopular in woods, is quite clear; the older lives have no wish to be stood in
    rows or at right angles. . . .

Athena's pragmatic spirit directed towards standing lives and things 'in rows or at right angles', towards order and tasks and agendas, becomes disconnected from soul and from earth. Then the goddess of the erect carriage and the long proud stride dries up like a withered stick. This is the dark side of the goddess who, because she sprang from the father's head, forgets the mother who conceived her. Yet Athena's deepest wisdom comes not from Zeus but from the ancient goddess of wisdom, 'the most knowing of the gods and men', her mother Metis whom Zeus devoured as soon as she became pregnant. He had been warned that Metis was destined to produce children whose wisdom would defeat the power of his lightning-bolts and challenge his supremacy. It is the wisdom not of the head but of the soul that Metis represents. And it is this deep, rooted wisdom that renews, which Athena denies proudly, even stridently, when she asserts: 'with all my heart I am my Father's child'.

By accepting her connection with Metis, Athena would rediscover a lost part of herself, preserved in the pre-Olympian myths about the Minoan shield goddess from whom Athena most likely descended. That goddess, as well as being a protective divinity, was a tree goddess and a snake goddess, both earthly symbols of eternal renewal. The ancient symbolism survived into classical times. Athena was the goddess of the olive tree, the sacred tree of Athens, and, even in the age of Pericles, Pheidias' famous statue of Athena Parthenos had a snake rearing up behind her shield and another coiled around her waist. Athena's very emblem, the owl, represents her dependence for strength and wisdom on the depths she denies. The owl is not only a wise bird but a night bird of death and darkness, 'associated with winged flight and spirit . . . the bringing of soul back into the upper air'.

Athena's rejection of her powerful, instinctual femininity and sexuality is part of her denial of the depths in her nature. When these are disowned, Athena becomes all head, and the darkness of this is there for all to see in the terrifying image of Medusa's head that the goddess wears on her breast – a head so horrible that those who see Medusa or are seen by her are turned to stone.

Today those modern Athenas dominated by their heads are busy living out the negative side of the goddess. Her dispassionate passion turns into coldness, aloofness, self-righteousness. Terrified of their vulnerability, they barricade themselves against life. Stubbornly self-sufficient, they run away from any relationship that threatens to disturb their boundaries.

Athena invented the bridle to harness horses, but she harnessed herself as well. The intrusion of sexuality in her well-ordered world turns the virgin goddess into a hag. The sight of Arachne's beautifully woven account of the lusty adventures of the gods reduced the reasonable and fair Athena to such a rage that she tore the cloth into threads, beat Arachne with her shuttle and

Fallen Doric columns, the remains of Athena's Archaic temple at Assos in Turkey, c. 530 BC.

drove her to hang herself. It is true that she saved the girl's life by loosening the rope, but the punishment was no less vicious: she transformed Arachne into a spider, condemned to hang on a thread, forever spinning her web. When Tiresias happened to see the goddess naked while she was bathing, she struck him blind. And when Medusa made love with Poseidon in a sanctuary dedicated to the goddess, Athena punished her by turning her into a horrifying snake-haired Gorgon. Athena found a place for the Furies in the city-state but not in herself.

When in 1879, Nora slammed the door on her 'Doll's House', Athena came alive in the heart of modern woman and has been gathering strength ever since:

> Athena was all I wanted to be and I gave my soul to her – self-confident and courageous, clear-eyed and strong, intelligent and accomplished, judicious and fair. I delighted in her ability to make full use of the given possibilities in any situation, in her gift for deep friendship unentangled with the confusions of passion, in her pleasure in struggle and challenge. Her dedication to the world of art and culture, of clear thought and realized accomplishment, were important testimony to me of how a woman might order her life.

One after another, masculine strongholds surrendered to Athena's strength and her power of persuasion, and once established, every advance was soundly defended. In the perennial pull between work and intimate relationships, femininity and assertiveness, intellect and sensuality, the modern Athenas chose work, assertiveness, intellect. Until, that is, recently when the signs of a new discontent began to appear symbolized by the baby boom among career women in their thirties and forties.

Freedom from the confines of a narrowly-defined femininity had turned out in many cases to be capitulation to the no less narrowly defined masculine values of our culture. Attendance at Athena's altar left deep needs neglected and powerful forces unacknowledged. Yet, paradoxically, there is no better place to begin the process of integration than at the altar of the grey-eyed goddess herself. In the more obscure elements of her myth, in the instinctiveness of the tree goddess and the snake goddess, in the intuitive wisdom of her mother Metis, even in her dark outbursts of passion, modern woman will find all the elements she needs to reclaim the parts of herself that she thought she had to leave behind in the 'Doll's House' in order to compete in a masculine world. In fact the task of integration belongs to Athena's essence. Under her patronage, women – and men too – can begin to weave together strength and vulnerability, creativity and nurturing, passion and discipline, pragmatism and intuition, intellect and imagination, until we claim them all, the masculine and the feminine, as part of our essence and expression.

Head of a Gorgon on the breast of a Caryatid at Eleusis, c. 30–25 BC.
'I turned your face around!
   It is my face.
That frozen rage is what I must
   explore –
Oh secret, self-enclosed and
   ravaged place!
That is the gift I thank Medusa
   for.'   MAY SARTON

LEFT Roman statue of Athena holding an owl, the bird of wisdom which was regarded as Athena herself in visible form, in the same way that Athena personified the inner wisdom of the heroes she protected and guided.

ABOVE Clay head of Athena, 490 BC. 'Homer meant by Athena *mind* and *intelligence*. And the maker of names appears to have had a singular notion about her, and indeed calls her by a still higher title, *divine intelligence*, as though he would say, This is she who has the mind of God.'
PLATO, *Cratylus*

LEFT Statue of Athena, with snakes and the Gorgon on her breast, from Lavinium in southern Italy. As well as being the goddess of wisdom and civilization, Athena was a tree goddess and a snake goddess, both earthly symbols of eternal renewal and a reminder of the goddess' dependence for true wisdom and strength on the instinctual depths that the tree and the snake represent.

ABOVE Marble statue of Athena, as it was renovated in 525 BC, from the Old Temple of Athena on the Acropolis in Athens. Athena fully aligns herself with the masculine order, but she breathes into it soul, mercy, wisdom. Her emergence, fully armed and independent, from Zeus' head, her total ease in the practical world of men whether on the battlefield or in the city, her inventive creativity, her involvement with law, justice and politics, all symbolize the great gift she can give modern women: the realization that creation and action are as inherently natural to a woman as to a man.

LEFT The Caryatid Porch of the Erechtheion on the Acropolis in Athens, c.410 BC.
'Goddess of Wisdom! here thy temple was
And is, despite of war and wasting fire,
And years that bade thy worship to expire....' BYRON

ABOVE View towards the Caryatid Porch of the Erechtheion
'And I in the trials of war where fighters burn for fame, will never endure the overthrow of Athens – all will praise her, victor city, pride of man.' AESCHYLUS, *Eumenides*

ABOVE Sculpture from the Parthenon in storage during the setting up of the Acropolis Museum after the Second World War.

PAGE 154 The Parthenon, 447–432 BC, embodies Athena at her fullest: male force and female receptivity, intellect and imagination, soaring towards the sky and enfolded in the arms of the earth.

PAGE 155 The temple of Athena Nike on the Acropolis, late 5th century BC.

RIGHT Mt Cyllene, the birthplace of Hermes. 'Muse, sing Hermes, son of Zeus and Maia, caretaker of Cyllene, and the sheepland Arcadia. . . .' *Homeric Hymn to Hermes*

PAGE 156 The Tholos at Delphi, 4th century BC.
'A motion and a spirit that impels
All thinking things, all objects of all thought. . . .'
WORDSWORTH

PAGE 157 Apollo's temple at Bassai, in an isolated and dramatic setting, was not discovered until 1765.

HERA

AMONG ALL THE OLYMPIANS, HERA has had the worst press. The scene was set by Homer who portrayed her as bitter, quarrelsome, jealous and possessive. And today, all these thousands of years later, it is the destructive side of Hera which dominates the emotional atmosphere that she conjures up.

Hera is not jealous: she is jealousy itself. She is not just the discontented wife: she is bitterness and frustration personified. She is the very image of clinging possessiveness, the eternal image of negative wifeness that we see in Edward Albee's *Who's Afraid of Virginia Woolf*, in James Joyce's Molly Bloom, in the offices of marriage counsellors, in the living rooms of our friends, in the bitter pillow-talk of our own bedrooms.

So long as Hera projects on her husband all her own unlived creativity, so long as she expects to find fulfilment exclusively in her role as Mrs Zeus, she creates her own betrayal and a marriage that is in a permanent state of war with brief interludes of peace in bed. Even loyalty, one of the most solid of the virtues that she embodies, turns into a yoke with which she tries to bind Zeus. Her much-vaunted fidelity becomes the martyr's demand to be endlessly acknowledged for her sacrifices. Instead of being a celebration of a freely given commitment, it expresses itself as a rejection of female sexuality. Hera's ultimate fidelity is not to the man but to the form. During one of their Olympian quarrels about whether men or women get more pleasure out of love-making, Zeus and Hera turned to Tiresias, the only human who had lived both as man and woman, for a conclusive answer. When he replied that women enjoyed love-making nine times as much as men, Hera became so furious that she struck him blind.

Raging and resentment are qualities of her very being and, sparked by jealousy, they drive her to frenetic activity. She is at her most resourceful and destructively creative when her jealousy demands revenge. She punishes

PAGE 158 Poseidon's kingdom.
'Will all great Neptune's ocean
    wash this blood
Clean from my hand? No, this
    my hand will rather
The multitudinous seas
    incarnadine,
Making the green one red.'
        SHAKESPEARE, *Macbeth*

PAGE 159 Poseidon's temple at
Sounion, the 'holy promontory
of Athens', mid 5th century BC.
'This relativity craze
In our contemporary life: There's
What gives space an importance
Found only in ourselves!'
        THOMAS MERTON

LEFT View from Perachora
across Lake Vouliagmene.
'To the ocean of His being the
spirit of life leads the streams of
action.'   *Isa Upanishad*

Echo for wilfully distracting her while she is trying to catch Zeus love-making with the nymphs by condemning her to repeat forever the last words uttered by others. She turns Io, one of Zeus' loves, into a cow, and when Zeus continues to love her, she has her driven out of Greece to Egypt by a gadfly. She sends two snakes into his cradle to strangle baby Herakles, the son of Zeus' infidelity with Alcmena; when he escapes by strangling the snakes instead, she goes on persecuting him until, in Euripides' *Herakles*, she drives him to madness and the murder of his wife and children. Even the birth of the three sons she conceived by herself, Ares, Hephaistos and Typhon, is motivated by anger – by the urge to show Zeus that she can produce a son alone who shall be glorious among the gods.

The emotions, and the chain of reactions they give rise to, may be overwhelmingly extravagant, but in them we can experience even more powerfully the destructive emotions and fantasies on which we expend so much energy in our own lives. All this darkness of raging and cruel vengeance has hidden Hera's light so effectively that it is at first hard to understand why she was so revered by the Greeks, why some of the most beautiful temples were dedicated in her honour, why, as Juno, she was above all other goddesses in Rome, why indeed she was worshipped as the goddess of sacred marriage.

It takes a fundamental shift of perspective to experience the light in Hera's polarity. The key to the shift is Hera's claiming back for herself the energy and the power that could not find expression in her role as wife and were instead turned self-destructively into jealousy, bitterness, resentment. Paradoxically, it is only when Hera stops seeking her definition in the role of wife that she embodies the essence of wife.

According to one of the most beautiful myths about the goddess, when she was no longer prepared to put up with Zeus' infidelities, she left him and returned to her birth-place in Euboea. They came together again but something is radically different between them. It is as if Hera had to distance herself from the relationship in order to connect with her own self-contained perfection and then, for the first time, meet her husband not in need but in fullness. 'Perhaps Hera had only really discovered her essential aloneness *within* the relationship, and could only learn what genuine relationship might be in solitude.' To persuade her to return, Zeus approaches Mt Cithaeron with a veiled female statue who is proclaimed as a local princess that the king of the gods is about to marry. Hera discovers the deceit and smiles. Filled with a secret, smiling wisdom that leaves no room for raging jealousy, she is reconciled to him, now ready for the deep marriage for which she has always longed.

In her heightened state, Hera embodies unconditional commitment to the

'Head of Hera', *c.* 590 BC. Filled with a secret smiling wisdom that leaves no room for raging jealousy, Hera is finally ready for the deep marriage for which she has always longed. Only when she stops seeking her definition in the role of Zeus' wife can she connect with her own self-contained perfection and then, for the first time, meet her husband not in need but in fullness.

primal relationship that marriage symbolizes. In fact she was the patroness of all stages of a woman's life in relation to man. She was known as Hera Parthenos (maiden), Hera Teleia (full-grown, complete), Hera Chera (widow). The word used to describe her state as wife shows that it was in the mystery of the sacred marriage that the goddess found her ultimate completion. Her three stages of transformation were identified by the Greeks with the three stages of the moon. She was the waxing moon as maiden, the full moon as fulfilled wife, the waning moon as abandoned, withdrawing woman.

'Hera is not the Great Mother but rather the spouse. That Hera is pre-eminently wife means that although she is a mother she is not mother as mother but mother as wife.' The other side of her destructively possessive aspect is a deep instinct to protect and nurture. Her protective aspect is sensitively evoked in the myth of her first loving encounter with Zeus. The god of gods sends a terrible storm to the mountain where Hera is sitting alone, turns himself into a cuckoo and descends trembling into her lap. The goddess takes the little bird in her arms and warms it by holding it tight against her breast.

Hera's protective strength manifests itself not only in her relationship with her husband but in her relationship to the community. Hera is a queen and the wider realm of things is as much her province as her family. Her attempt to make communities both of Olympos and the earth is an expression of the passionate concern she embodies for the communal life, for the whole. Aphrodite's passions may move us more readily in their intensity and surrender to the moment, but societies cannot survive without Hera's steadfast commitment to the values and institutions on which they are founded.

We see Hera at work in all the women who devote a large part of their lives to running schools, hospitals, charities and churches. And we also see negative Hera at work when their social concern becomes mechanical and disconnected from the spirit that inspired it, or when they use it as a substitute for following their own life-giving energy where it leads them.

In the same way, the women who identify themselves with their husbands' work can either find in that supportive identification true fulfilment or hide dark resentment and frustration in their role as the 'power behind the throne'. Hera had her own 'golden throne' on Olympos, and when the modern Heras rediscover their own thrones and recreate their own kingdoms they will redeem the role of wife from its present discredited state and resolve Hera's central ambivalence. Until then Hera will remain buried in the tensions and anxieties of our marriages and our most intimate relationships, working her destructive will, possessive and possessed.

RIGHT View from the fortress of Palamidi at Nauplion. Hera appeared to the Argive women once a year. She bathed in the spring flowing through the foothills and emerged with her virginity renewed – One-in-Herself, the Celestial Virgin.

PAGE 166 Hera's temple at Olympia, early 6th century BC. 'Here I sing of Hera, she has a golden throne. . . . She is the sister, she is even the wife of Zeus the thunderer. She is glorious, all the gods on vast Olympos revere her, they honour her even equal to Zeus the lover of lightning.'
Homeric Hymn to Hera

PAGE 167 Typhon, *c.* 570 BC. Hera's fatherless son was a three-bodied monster with a hundred burning snake-heads – an expression of Hera's rage at Zeus and part of her struggle against him. He made war on Zeus as soon as he was fully grown, and he was only finally subjugated when the king of the gods trapped him under the island of Sicily where his breath created the flames of Mt Etna.

HESTIA

HESIOD CALLED HER THE CHIEF OF ALL GODDESSES, Zeus' sister, Cronos' and Rhea's first-born. A *Homeric Hymn* tells us that 'she has her place in the centre of the house to receive the best in offerings'. The goddess of the hearth, of the centre to which life returns to be replenished, was honoured in every household and in all the temples of all the gods, but there is not a word about her in Homer, no myths that revolved around her, no images of her, no statues in her temples. Her name, according to Plato, means 'the essence of things', and since she is the essence of everything that moves and flows and has life and personality, she is herself the most anonymous, the least personal of all the goddesses. She was worshipped as the centre: the centre of the city, the centre of the house, even the centre of the centre of the world, the omphalos, the navel, at Delphi.

Hestia's public function remained important right down to Roman times when she was worshipped as the goddess Vesta: 'The continuous fire of Vesta was indeed "the heart of Rome" and hence one of the guarantees of the city being rooted in earth, of its permanence in history; it assured the Romans of stability and permanence in their place on earth.' The sacred fire that burned in her temple was tended by the Vestals, the virgin priestesses of the goddess, and so strong was the identification of her living flame with the life and safety of the city that neglect of the sacred fire was punished with death.

Hestia's fire, her life energy, burned for the city but, even more important, it burned for each individual, each human soul. She was the centre on which the city's solid foundation was built, and she was the bedrock of man's being, manifesting 'the almost irresistible compulsion and urge to *become what one is*, just as every organism is driven to assume the form that is characteristic of its nature'. It is, therefore, not surprising that when our outer activities take over and dominate our existence, Hestia becomes the forgotten goddess. She is not about striving and straining, competing and succeeding; she is about being. Christ's admonition, 'Seek ye first the kingdom of God and all things shall be added unto you', could have come, just as naturally, from Hestia's mouth.

There is a deep peace that surrounds the goddess when I conjure her up in my mind's eye, a fullness and a smiling acceptance that represent, as only Hermes among the rest of the pantheon does, the essence of unconditional loving. Her fire warms, kindles, illuminates. 'She sees all things by her light that never fails.' She is the gathering point, the source and the centre that sustain our place of return, 'the builder of the house so that the soul may dream in peace.... The soul gone astray, is a soul without psychic connection to this goddess and her centredness.... "Off base", "Off centre", "unable to find a place", "can't settle down", "spaced out", and "off the wall", are related to Hestian values and remind the wanderer of her power to bring the soul into a state of dwelling.'

The house that Hestia builds provides the boundaries for our soul, protecting it from the invasion of the outside world and protecting us from the chaos of chance happenings, from triviality and futility. 'Now even as the mind of god is nourished by reason and knowledge', wrote Plato in *Phaedrus*, 'so also is it with every soul that has a care to receive her proper food; wherefore, when at last she has beheld being, she is well content, and contemplating truth she is nourished and prosperous, until the heaven's revolution brings her back full circle.' Hestia, the guardian of our homecoming, nourishes the depths of our being, leavens our lives and provides a centre in which to contain our disconnected experiences. The essence of the forgotten goddess has a profound relevance for modern man caught in 'doing' and activity, not in the sense of denying 'doing' and activity, but so as to pass from our identification with our external puppet self to the realization of our larger being; from our mechanistic existence to a connection with the still centre in which life's journey is contained.

ARES

ARES, AS THE EMBODIMENT OF AGGRESSION, has been one of the strongest forces working through human history. He is Olympos' 'Action Man', the god of war and strife, the restless and turbulent lover, thriving on conflict and rejoicing in the delight of battle. In Ares we see our own aggression raw and bloody, before civilization tempered or repressed it and, of course, we loathe what we see. Ares was the most hated among the gods. Homer calls him a 'butcher'; heroes rejoice in having escaped 'the fury of the ruthless god'; Athena berates him as a 'blockhead' and a 'maniac'.

Athena and Ares represent two different aspects of aggression. Athena fought to defend, to protect; she fought with strategy and clear intention. Ares is our primordial rage allowed full sway, our hot-blooded energy shooting out lustfully with no thought or restraint.

> Lord Ares, yours is the din of arms, and ever bespattered by blood
> you find joy in killing and in the fray of battle, O hateful one.

In the fray of battle, it is clear-headed Athena who triumphs over Ares' frenzy. When in the *Iliad* Diomedes, at Athena's instigation, wounds the god with his spear, he lets out a bellow as loud as nine or ten thousand men and runs to Zeus for comfort. The father of gods is unmoved: 'You turncoat, don't come to me and whine. There is nothing you enjoy so much as quarrelling and fighting: which is why I hate you more than any god on Olympos.'

Whining and cowardice are the underside of Ares' strident aggression, the unheroic side of his nature which he never dares confront. And Athena's victory over him, both through Diomedes and at another stage in the Trojan War when she lays him low with a stone, is a powerful symbol of the superiority of conscious heroic striving over the ravaging impulses of

Marble statue of a Spartan warrior, once thought to represent Leonidas, hero of the battle of Thermopylae, 490–480 BC.
'Ares, lord of strife,
Who doth the swaying scales of battle hold,
War's money-changer, giving dust for gold,
Sends back, to hearts that held them dear,
Scant ash of warriors, wept with many a tear. . . .'
AESCHYLUS, *Agamemnon*

mindless aggression. When, furious and uncontrollable over his son's death on the battlefield of Troy, he is ready to disobey Zeus' order that no god should fight in the war, it is Athena who stops him. Snatching the helmet from his head, the bronze spear from his hand and the shield from his shoulder, she literally disarms him: brute battle-rage has to be transformed by wisdom for civilization to be born and to survive.

After the upsurges of our Ares' nature resulting in the great wars of this century and the haunting possibility of complete annihilation through a nuclear holocaust, the need for a force to temper primordial aggression, the need for Athena, is more urgent than ever before. Ares tears asunder the order of culture and civilization; Athena and that ultimate symbol of rational consciousness, Apollo, bind, temper, harmonize.

In the myths of Ares' childhood, both Hera, his mother, and his tutor Priapus teach him dancing – an artful activity that guides some of the young god's feverish energy away from warfare and conflict. Ares' prodigious energy and will to power are not in themselves destructive; it is the channel into which they are directed which determines whether they propel the warmonger, the criminal and the outlaw or the hero, the builder of cities, the pioneer. In astrology, Ares corresponds to the planet Mars which represents the thrust for unrestrained self-assertion, an aggressive determination to win, a voracious ambition for power. In its positive aspect, though, unrestrained self-assertion turns into creative assertiveness, aggression into courage, the ambition for power into the quest for achievement. Ares' spirit is the spirit behind the competitiveness of rugged individualism, the spirit that drives man to win and gives him the strength and perseverance to do so, the spirit that thrusts him into adventure and new conquests. We see it clearly at work in the business pioneer, in the athlete breaking new records, in the man who 'makes it' against all odds and survives despite all adversity.

So Ares has dominated our century both in war and in peace. Now, in the growing trend away from aggressive acquisition, fierce competitiveness and the endless struggle to surpass the Joneses, our age is revolting against him. It is to the myth of Ares' passionate relationship with Aphrodite, his lusty aggression creatively united with love, that our exhausted century can look for a new beginning. The four children they produced symbolize the two aspects of their natures. The union between Ares' elemental aggression and Aphrodite's unbridled sexuality produced Deimos (panic) and Phobos (fear); the union of his life-giving instinctuality and her binding power of love gave birth to Eros and Harmonia.

In the 'quality-of-life' movements, in the search for alternatives to the technological world-view, in the emphasis on participation and the community, in the flood of books and workshops on self-fulfilment, we see

Ares fighting the giants during the battle between the giants and the gods, from the north frieze of the Siphnian Treasury at Delphi, c. 525 BC.

the yearning for Eros and Harmony to balance the competitive, adversary, ruthlessly individualistic elements in our age of Ares.

'Life persists in the middle of destruction,' said Gandhi. 'Therefore there must be a higher law than that of destruction. Only under that law would well-ordered society be intelligible and life worth living.' The law of aggression and destruction is the law of Ares in his darkest aspect – the law that reduces life to the jungle. The quest for a higher law is the manifestation of Ares' highest nature – a passionate instinct for life that does, indeed, persist in the middle of destruction.

HEPHAISTOS

Looking towards the Acropolis from the temple of Hephaistos in Athens.
'Sing, clear-voiced Muse, of Hephaistos famed for his skill. With bright-eyed Athena he taught men glorious crafts throughout the world – men who before used to dwell in caves in the mountains like wild beasts. But now that they have learned crafts through Hephaistos the famed worker, easily they live a peaceful life in their own houses the whole year round.'

Homeric Hymn to Hephaistos

HEPHAISTOS IS THE ONLY OLYMPIAN WHO WORKS – the other gods plot, manipulate events, make things happen, but they do not work in the consuming sense that our modern era understands the word. So it is not surprising that on the eve of the Industrial Age it was this aspect of Hephaistos, and his Roman equivalent Vulcan, that excited the imagination of Tintoretto and Velazquez, Rubens and Van Dyck. They show him toiling at the forge, busily at work in his workshop in the womb of the earth.

Hephaistos is the embodiment of man's unquenched creativity – the creativity that forged the bridge between our primordial dependence on nature and our industrial world. He is the symbol of endless resourcefulness and prodigious productivity. He built the magnificent Olympian palaces; he made the golden shoes with which the gods trod the air or the water and moved from place to place with the speed of the wind, or even of thought; he shod with brass the celestial steeds; he made Achilles' intricately wrought shield, Athena's spear, Apollo's and Artemis' arrows, Agamemnon's sceptre, Demeter's sickle, jewels for Zeus' lovers. He made the first self-propelled objects – tripods, tables and chairs that could move in and out of the celestial halls by themselves; he made the first robots, fully endowed with artificial intelligence – golden maidservants that, Homer tells us, 'looked like real girls and could not only speak and use their limbs, but were endowed with intelligence and trained in handiwork by the immortal gods'. He even made, in the likeness of Aphrodite, Pandora whom Zeus sent to earth to plague men.

Hephaistos' creative gift is solidly grounded on the earth, and there is magic as well as magnificence in what he produces. In his workshop he is supreme, unrivalled, but like the modern man who identifies himself exclusively with his work, he is at a total loss outside it. He was born

175

deformed, with his feet turned backwards, making it difficult to walk except with a forward-rolling movement. But his crippledness in no way affected his work – his monumental capacity to produce and create. It was only in his relationships that it became an issue, especially in his relationship to the feminine. He is lost in a world of intimacy where he cannot use axe or forge to create. Indeed his lameness is the physical manifestation of an emotional crippledness that invites rejection. And rejection is the leitmotif pervading his involvement with women. It starts with his rejection by Hera who gave birth to him parthenogenically and, appalled by his deformity, flung him out of Olympos. And it colours from the beginning his relationship with Aphrodite, the goddess of love and beauty who becomes his wife.

It is a marriage born not of love but of blackmail. Aphrodite was the prize Hephaistos demanded from Zeus for setting Hera free. His revenge on the mother who rejected him was to send her an exquisite, golden throne with invisible chains that bound her inextricably. Consternation reigned on Olympos, and an urgent message was sent to Hephaistos to come back and free his mother. I have no mother, replies the divine craftsman, and refuses to leave his subterranean workshop. Ares is sent to force him to Olympos but has to retreat, defeated, before his brother's flames. Then, on the principle that only a trickster can catch a trickster, Dionysos is dispatched to Hephaistos' underworld. There the god of the vine meets the god of the forge, and ecstasy wins over determination. Dionysos introduces Hephaistos to wine and, through wine, to an unfamiliar part of himself. Having got him ecstatically drunk, he sets him on a mule and leads him to Olympos as if in a triumphant procession – a favourite scene of vase painters in antiquity. Confronted with his enthroned and enchained mother, Hephaistos sobers up and refuses to release her until the gods promise him Aphrodite for his wife. He forces the goddess into marriage but he cannot force her into love.

The free spirit of passion that Aphrodite embodies cannot be compelled. And once again Hephaistos has to resort to the world of mechanical contrivances, the only world he really understands, this time to catch Aphrodite and Ares love-making in his own bed. It is one of the most beautiful and deeply human myths in the *Odyssey*:

> When he heard the galling truth he went straight to his workshop with his heart full of evil thoughts, laid his great anvil on the smithy and forged a chain network that could neither be broken nor undone, so as to keep them prisoners forever. His fury with Ares inspired him as he worked, and when the snare was finished he went to the room where his bed was laid and threw the netting right around the bedposts. A number of further lengths were attached to the rafters overhead and hung down light as a gossamer and quite invisible even to the blessed gods. It was a masterful piece of cunning work.

Now the situation becomes pure Feydeau farce. As soon as Hephaistos has laid the invisible chains, he pretends to leave for Lemnos, and no sooner has he gone than Ares appears. Aphrodite, desiring 'nothing better than to sleep with him', leads him to her marriage bed. Hephaistos' chains close instantly upon them and, too late, they find out that there is no escape. The betrayed husband arrives, wild with rage:

> His shouts brought the gods trooping to the house with the bronze door. Up came Poseidon, the Earthshaker; Hermes, the bringer of luck; and the archer king, Apollo; but the goddesses, constrained by feminine modesty, all stayed at home. There they stood then, in front of the doors ... and when they caught sight of Hephaistos' clever device a fit of uncontrollable laughter seized these happy gods. .... except Poseidon, who was not amused, but kept urging the great smith Hephaistos to free Ares from the net. 'Let them go,' he insisted: 'and I promise you that he himself shall make full and proper atonement, as required by you, in the presence of the immortal gods.'

The atonement Hephaistos demands is the return of the gifts he had given Zeus to marry Aphrodite. He turns from the love he cannot have to the golden material objects he can. He can use his skill to bind women in traps but lacks the spirit to create bonds of relationship.

Outside his workshop, the god becomes the fool. In the *Odyssey*, the blind bard Demodocus amuses King Alcinous' court by singing the tale of Aphrodite making a cuckold of her husband. In the *Iliad*, the gods themselves burst out laughing as he clumsily bustles up and down the hall to serve them nectar from a huge bowl. The master craftsman who achieves perfection in his artifacts and mechanical inventions completely misses the mark when it comes to flesh and blood relationships. In the myth of his pursuit of Athena he literally misses the mark when he excitedly and impetuously tries to make love to her. At the moment of climax she pushes him aside and he ejaculates against her thigh instead. His semen falls on the ground and impregnates Gaia, the Goddess Earth, producing Erichthonios, the man from whom the Athenians claim their heritage.

Modern man is living out both sides of the Hephaistos archetype. He has created the supreme technological civilization and, at the same time, he has spawned a whole industry of sexual manuals, sexual aids and psycho-therapeutic tools. He has created artificial intelligence on earth and has sent man to the moon, but he can hardly make love without the help of Masters and Johnson, or maintain a loving relationship without recourse to the technologists of intimacy.

DEMETER

DEMETER IS MOTHER — EARTH MOTHER, ELEMENTAL MOTHER, raging mother, grieving mother, adoring mother, clinging mother. It is impossible to think of her except in relationship to Persephone, her daughter. In most ancient sculptures of Demeter and Persephone, they are seen looking deeply into each other's eyes, and the secret they share through their penetrating gaze is at the heart of Demeter's myth. 'Every mother contains her daughter in herself, and every daughter her mother, and every woman extends backwards into her mother and forwards into her daughter.'

The myth of Demeter and Persephone is one of the richest, most profound and most moving in all Greek mythology. Persephone, who is also known as Kore, which in modern Greek still means daughter, is playing with her friends in the fields, innocent and carefree, when she suddenly comes upon a narcissus 'awesome to behold for both gods and men'. As she reaches to pick the flower with the intoxicating scent, the earth opens beneath her and, resisting and weeping, she is carried off to the Underworld by Hades. 'And the mountain peaks', the *Homeric Hymn* tells us, 'echoed with her immortal voice, and the depths of the sea, and her noble mother heard her. A sharp pain seized her heart.' She tore the diadem from her head, covered herself in dark sheets of mourning and for nine days and nine nights she wandered the earth without eating, drinking or bathing, in search of her daughter.

> . . . And forth again
> Among the wail of midnight winds, and cried
> 'Where is my loved one? Wherefore do ye wail?'
> And out from all the night an answer shrill'd,
> 'We know not, and we know not why we wail.'
> I climb'd on all the cliffs of all the seas,
> And ask'd the waves that moan about the world

Demeter, Triptolemos and Kore, *c.*440–430 BC. 'Demeter and Kore, mother and daughter, extend the feminine consciousness upwards and downwards – and widen out the narrowly conscious mind bound in space and time, giving it intimations of a greater and more comprehensive personality which has a share in the eternal course of things. . . .' C. G. JUNG

'Where do ye make your moaning for my child?'
And round from all the world the voices came,
'We know not, and we know not why we moan.'
'Where?' and I stared from every eagle peak.
I thridded the black heart of all the woods,
I peer'd thro' tomb and cave, and in the storms
Of autumn swept across the city, and heard
The murmur of their temples chanting me,
Me, me, the desolate mother! 'Where?' – and turn'd,
And fled by many a waste, forlorn of man,
And grieved for man thro' all my grief for thee, –
The jungle rooted in his shatter'd hearth,
The serpent coil'd about his broken shaft,
The scorpion crawling over naked skulls; –
I saw the tiger in the ruin'd fane
Spring from his fallen God, but trace of thee
I saw not; and far on, and following out
A league of labyrinthine darkness, came
On three gray heads beneath a gleaming rift.
'Where?' and I heard one voice from all the three,
'We know not, for we spin the lives of men,
And not of gods, and know not why we spin!
There is a Fate beyond us.' Nothing knew.

On the tenth day, Hecate, who had also heard Persephone's cries, came to Demeter and together they went to the god Helios, the sun, who told them that it was Zeus who, with the help of Gaia, the Goddess Earth, produced the narcissus with a hundred heads that beguiled Persephone; it was he who gave her to Hades, his own brother, for his wife.

. . . Then I, Earth-Goddess, cursed the Gods of heaven.
I would not mingle with their feasts; to me
Their nectar smack'd of hemlock on the lips,
Their rich ambrosia tasted aconite.
That man, that only lives and lives an hour,
Seemed nobler than their hard eternities.
My quick tears kill'd the flower, my ravings hush'd
The bird, and lost in utter grief I fail'd
To send my life thro' olive-yard and vine
And golden-grain, my gift to helpless man.
Rain-rotten died the wheat, the barley spears
Were hollow-husk'd, the leaf fell, and the Sun,
Pale at my grief, drew down before his time
Sickening, and Aetna kept her winter snow.

The shrine of the Great Gods on the island of Samothrace. Chief among the pre-Olympian deities to whom the shrine was dedicated was the Great Mother, Gaia, closely identified with Demeter.

The goddess who brought plenty to men was now letting everything wither and die and, withered herself, she spent her days as a nursemaid at the palace of the king of Eleusis. In her grief and rage she would have wiped out the whole race of men had Zeus not interceded. First he sent Iris to implore her to return to Olympos and restore fertility to the earth, then he sent out 'every one of the blessed gods', and when all had failed to move her heart, he finally relented and sent Hermes to Hades to tell him that he must let Persephone return to the daylight world. As they were parting, Hades offered her a pomegranate seed to eat, and Persephone, who so far had eaten nothing in the Underworld, took the seed and ate it. To eat food in the Underworld meant that you had to return, and from that time and for all eternity, Persephone had to spend one third of the year in misty darkness with Hades. The rest of the year's cycle she would spend with her mother and the immortal gods – and the earth would bloom with fragrant flowers and all fruits and grains and crops. 'Everywhere her energy was stirring, pushing, bursting forth into tender greenery and pale young petals. Animals shed all fur and rolled in the fresh, clean grass while birds sang out: 'Persephone returns! Persephone returns!' But for one third of the year's cycle everything would be bare and fallow and bleak.

The myth ends with Demeter teaching the rulers of Eleusis her rites and her mysteries that for a thousand years were celebrated in deep secrecy as the ultimate revelation of the spiritual life of antiquity. The fertility goddess and earth mother of the myth's beginnings has been transformed by the end into the goddess of the highest mysteries of man's divine nature. Grain, and especially corn, is Demeter's earthly gift, but the grain that sinks to the earth and returns points beyond itself to a universal symbol actualized through the sacred gift of the Eleusinian Mysteries: man's death to his mundane self and his rebirth in his divine essence. 'Verily I say unto you, except a corn of wheat fall into the ground and die, it abideth alone; but if it die, it bringeth forth much fruit.'

In becoming the goddess of the highest esoteric mysteries, Demeter, far from denying the concrete, material world over which she rules, adds another dimension of significance to it and spiritualizes it. This dimension is personified in the myth by Hades, the god of the Underworld, the god of the unconscious. And nature, in the form of the older Earth Mother, Gaia, recognizes the necessity for the violent abduction that will connect the upper world with the unseen and the invisible and conspires with Zeus and Hades to bring this about by growing the glorious narcissus that seduces Persephone.

So long as Demeter resists the depths, she grieves and rages and withers. When she can finally accept the deeper reality that lies beneath the surface,

The Kistophoros Caryatid, *c.*30–25 BC. On her head she supports a sacred basket decorated with wheat and poppies.
'... and bless
Their garner'd Autumn also, reap
    with me,
Earth-mother, in the harvest
    hymns of Earth
The worship which is Love....'
TENNYSON

the depth potential as 'a seed in each moment of life', the earth blooms and
rejoices, and out of her festivals of agriculture and the changing of the seasons
and her own wanderings and pain, the Eleusinian Mysteries are born.

They were divided into the Greater and the Lesser Mysteries, the Lesser
held in the spring, the Greater in September. The Greater Mysteries lasted
for nine days, the nine days of Demeter's wandering and grief. The initiates'
procession from Athens to Eleusis, the fasting, the sacred pageant dealing
with the story of Persephone's abduction, the period of withdrawal and
purification, were all re-enactments of the myth symbolically experienced
by each initiate. The sacred marriage in which the rites culminated was the
union of the earth with the divine, the material with the spiritual; it led to the
birth of the divine child who is the 'whole' – the redeeming symbol through
which are reconciled the warring opposites of love and rage, earthliness and
spirituality, rootedness and wandering, hiddenness and openness, life and
death.

Demeter's quest for her lost child is, on another level, her longing for the
divine child that is symbolically born at the end of the Eleusinian Mysteries –
the divine child within, that we desperately need to reconstruct the lost
wholeness in ourselves and end the pain of separation that is part of our
incarnation on earth. Whether caught in our busy world of activity like
Demeter, or in the surface life of a playful paradise like Persephone, life
demands that we be shaken into awareness. And it will use anything, the
myth tells us, including abandonment, rage and loss, to move us in the
direction of the inner world and steer us into consciousness and wholeness.

The call to reunite ourselves with the lost child within, the lost maiden – what Jung called the 'anima' – can no longer be stifled. Sometimes in the strangest guises, it is nevertheless everywhere in evidence. In the musical *Hair*, the refrain of the song Donna ('Oh Donna, Oh Donna, Donna/ Looking for My Donna') evokes the yearning for a 'once upon a time' sixteen-year-old virgin called Donna. 'It is as if the virgin calls us *to* ourselves, to be true to something within ourselves which cannot be shared with others.' It is a call in the middle of our ephemeral, fragmented lives to connect with that virginal, childlike part of ourselves through which we can participate in the eternal course of life. Our defence against the divine depths leads to the grieving and the raging that form such a large part of Demeter's myth and of modern life. And until there is acceptance and understanding, suffering feeds upon itself and all sense of essence and significance is lost.

This defensive clinging to the upper world, to the surface world of activity, is Demeter's negative aspect. It also manifests itself as clinging possessively either to a child or to whatever has been nurtured like a child, whether it is an institution, a project or an idea. Demeter, in her smothering, witch's aspect, would rather destroy what she has given birth to than let it develop independently of herself. In her positive aspect as the elemental mother and the 'eternal feminine leading above', Demeter embodies the highest mysteries of man's nature and the alternating cycles of plenty and fallowness contained in nature and in human nature – in the change of the seasons, in all human activity, and in the ebb and flow of our emotional and spiritual lives.

HADES

HADES, THE GOD OF DEATH, is today the hardest god to relate to. In our proudly rationalist society, death, our life's only certainty and ultimate mystery, is an embarrassment, a break in efficiency, a failure in man's conquest of nature. Hades teaches us acceptance of death as part of life and, even more important, he teaches us the need, in Socrates' words, to 'practise death' daily. Practising death is evaluating the lesser in our lives in terms of the greater, our passions and pleasures and ambitions in terms of what is invisible and hidden from our eyes yet underlies our existence, enriching it with meaning and depth. Hades' other name was Pluto, which in Greek means wealth, riches, and the god's invisible fullness was symbolized by the image of the cornucopia that he held in his hands, overflowing with fruits and vegetables or with jewels, gems, gold and silver.

In Homer's cosmic geography, Hades was the name of the physical realm of the Underworld as well as the name of its god. And there were many caves in Greece – on the River Styx, in Lebadeia, at Cape Tainaron – that were believed to be actual entrances to Hades. In our own lives there are many dark moments that can act as 'entrances' into Hades' realm, as opportunities to descend to the depths where we can digest our experiences and turn them into the raw material of our constant transformations. 'All descents provide entry into different levels of consciousness and can enhance life creatively. ... All of them can serve as initiations. Meditation and dreaming and active imagination are modes of descent.'

Hades is the god presiding over our descents, investing the darkness in our lives, our depressions, our anxieties, our emotional upheavals and our grief with the power to bring illumination and renewal. A very active woman described in her journal her descent from the established pattern of her life as 'a slow decaying of all the "shoulds"'. . . . I have had to accept that slowness

A young nobleman on his horse on a funerary vase, c. 420 BC. 'They are the souls destined for new bodies, and there at Lethe's stream they drink of its waters which give release from anxiety and memory of the past. . . . When all these souls have completed a cycle of a thousand years, God summons them to the stream of Lethe in a mighty procession so that, forgetful of the past, they may begin to wish to be reincarnated.' VIRGIL

and the destruction of what I thought was me. There is always the fear that once I sacrifice the old, social, competent me, I will be dead. Yet in this depressed place, where I have felt inertia in the embrace of uttermost matter, like cement holding me, there has been an unbinding of energy.'

Psychology, literature, religion are full of instances of what is hidden rising from below and filling our life with darkness. St John of the Cross talked of the 'dark night of the soul'. Today we label the darkness, the heaviness that unaccountably overwhelms us, depression – something to be relieved with pills, drowned in alcohol or escaped from in activity. But many are beginning to discover the god in the 'depression', to see new domains of new possibilities revealed through the disturbance of our plans and of the personalities we have embraced as ourselves. Death is a prerequisite of every rebirth. As the seed must die to be born again, so a part of us must die before we can give birth to the reality hidden in our depths.

What we are in the process of becoming is infinitely greater than what we are, which is why the self that is growing in us but into which we have not yet grown can never rest content with our present and, by definition, inferior actuality. When we recognize this, we can accept the death contained in our depressions, our losses, our endings, our defeats, as life's way of forcing us to take the next step in our evolution. 'Life becomes relieved of having to be a vast defensive arrangement against psychic realities.' And we can accept Hades/Pluto in our midst as the god both of our literal death and of our daily deaths and rebirths, of our descents into the Underworld – in the footsteps of Herakles and Dionysos, Aeneas and Odysseus – to bring forth more and more of our invisible riches. He stirs our numbness to pain, he disturbs our safe, comfortable, arrested existence, he breaks up the old patterns we cling to, and through the darkness leads us to a deeper seeing and a richer, more resonant being.

What the initiates discovered in the mysteries of ancient Greece is that the god who would forever bring loss and suffering also engendered good and compelled or even pushed men towards the fulfilment of their destinies. Hades enters our lives creatively unless we ignore the claim on us of the invisible powers that he embodies. In our solar system Pluto is the outermost planet. In our lives Hades/Pluto represents the forces in us that reach furthest and deepest, urging us to return, this time consciously, to the roots of life. Pluto, the planet, discovered in 1930, was the last planet to come to the surface of man's awareness. And Pluto, the god, traditionally excluded from the pantheon of the principal divinities, is the god we most urgently need to discover today, allowing him to guide us below the threshold of our narrow existence and sacrificing to him some of the energy we have for centuries been devoting to our outer projects, desires and activities.

Funerary *kouros*, 550–540 BC. The dark moments in our lives can act as 'entrances' into Hades' realm, as opportunities to descend to the depths where we find meaning in our wounds, our hurts and our depressions in the service of a greater, a richer, a more conscious life.

HERMES

TO ASK WHO IS YOUR FAVOURITE GOD is as vain a question as to ask which is your favourite Mozart opera. Yet we all have our favourite among his operas, and I certainly have my favourite among the gods. *The Magic Flute* is my favourite Mozart opera – indeed, my favourite opera – and Hermes my favourite god. Only recently did I become aware of the connection. *The Magic Flute* is about the voyage, the adventure, of a soul through different realms, different tests, through love, fear, pain and joy. Hermes is the guide of our voyage and the guardian-spirit of our adventure.

If I close my eyes and try to conjure up Hermes, I see motion: winged sandals, winged words, wings on his low-crowned hat, wings on his magic wand, the gods' messenger who 'flies as fleet as thought', the driver of the sun's chariot, the guide to the Underworld, 'the wayfarer', 'swift-running', 'swift-footed'. My mind quivers with the epithets, the images, the representations of unchained energy.

I cannot write about Hermes impersonally. He is the first god who moved me, who opened my heart to the mystery of the gods and the extraordinariness of the ordinary. He is the god of the unexpected, of luck, of coincidences, of synchronicity. 'Hermes has entered in our midst', the ancient Greeks would say when a sudden silence entered the room, descended on the conversation, introduced into the gathering another dimension. Whenever things seem fixed, rigid, 'stuck', Hermes introduces fluidity, motion, new beginnings – and the confusion that almost inevitably precedes new beginnings.

He is the primordial divine child, the child that if man is lucky he never outgrows. He was born of Zeus and the nymph Maia in an Arcadian cave and he was admitted into the Olympian hierarchy immediately, as a child. His divine innocence bears the closest connection to the origins of life and to

Hermes carrying the baby Dionysos to the nymphs who were to bring him up, *c.* 350–340 BC. Hermes carries in himself the primordial divine child, the child that if man is lucky he never outgrows. Hermes' world, like that of Dionysos, is the shifting world of reality that includes endless transformations.

immortality. And as a child, the *Homeric Hymn* tells us, he introduces childlike qualities – mischievousness, spontaneity, delight – into the Olympian order.

> Born in the morning, he played the lyre by afternoon, and by evening had stolen the cattle of the Archer Apollo. . . . As he stepped over the threshold of the high-roofed cave, he found a tortoise there and gained endless delight. So it was Hermes who first made the tortoise a singer. . . . The son of Zeus, the helper, looked at it, burst out laughing and said this: 'What a great sign, what a help this is for me! I won't ignore it. Hello there, little creature, dancing up and down, companion at festivals, how exciting it is to see you.'

First there is the laughter, then the attention to the signs life gives us. Hermes stumbles over the tortoise and makes the first lyre out of its shell. 'Few of us automatically honour the chance find, the stumbled-over discovery that makes life-music.' Hermes' world is a magical world full of signs and significance. He was the god who first gave me, as a child, a sense of the miraculous all around me. I 'grew up' and lost it. I got caught in rational plans, will-power, the need to control circumstances, to impose certainties in my life, to even things out to what my more Hermetic sister called 'a vanilla grey'. And then, by rediscovering Hermes, I recreated his spirit: fluid, trusting, open to signs, coincidences, the unforeseeable and the unexpected. 'He charms the eyes of men or awakens whom he wills', Homer tells us in the *Odyssey*. Introducing the element of the unexpected into our lives is one of the means he uses to spur us out of sleeping wakefulness and to break through the rigidities and confinement of habits and conventions.

We learn as much about Hermes from his appellations and epithets as from his myths. He was known as the god 'of the gateway', the god 'dwelling at the gate', and the unique gate he opened up for me led to the hidden world of meanings beneath the surface of the obvious. He was also known as the guide of dreams and the *psithyristis*, a word which still in modern Greek means the whisperer; and he taught me to listen to the inner whisperings that tend to get drowned in the mind's cacophony, and to value and respect my dreams.

Along with our first image of Hermes as a divine child we have the view of him as an old man with a beard represented in the phallus-shaped stone pillar, the herm. It is one more paradox in a divinity made of them. He was considered the demon or spirit of the most primitive form of herm, the stone heap, and even now in certain mountainous parts of Europe the traveller who wants to invoke good luck will add a stone to the pile already there beside the road. Stone has always represented that great *forever*, outside space, time and the constant change to which we are relentlessly subjected. And the

The Palestra, or wrestling ground, at Olympia, 3rd century BC. Hermes, who 'flies as fleet as thought', 'swift-footed', 'swift-running', was considered the god of racing and wrestling. Both his appellations and his images – winged sandals, wings on his low-crowned hat, wings on his magic wand – are representations of the unchained energy he embodies.

god, whose myths portray him mostly in flight, frequently vanishing before our eyes, is also represented in the symbol of the greatest, most permanent and irreducible reality – the stone.

For many years I was uncomfortable with this aspect of Hermes. My mind would not allow my god of motion and freedom to be imprisoned in stone. But the gods cannot be tidied up to fit our understanding, and I have gradually learned that when a part of a myth or an aspect of a god does not fit my perception, the answer is not to dismiss the paradox, but to enlarge my perception to include it. So when I thought I had caught Hermes as spirit in motion, he emerged as matter in stone. And with the unexpectedness Hermes would have relished, it was in the world of modern science that I discovered the key to this double nature of an ancient god. Matter, Einstein showed us, is condensed energy, energy convertible to matter. What the increasingly surrealistic discoveries of post-Newtonian science reveal is that mass and energy, particle and wave, are merely two aspects of the same reality. Once again, Hermes takes us by surprise and, through modern science, he is teaching us the same lesson he taught us through ancient myth: what appear as opposites, as distinct dimensions, are in fact one, expressions of the same reality, fired by the same breath. Which is why he is the god of connections, bridging realms and dissolving frontiers: between earth and the Underworld, men and gods, life and death.

Every other god has a centre, a particular colour in the spectrum, determined for all time, a special imprint on an aspect of our lives and ourselves. Hermes' centre is everywhere, part of an ever-expanding spiral, and every colour in the cosmic rainbow is his. He excludes nothing and illuminates everything. He is equally at home on Olympos and in the subterranean depths. He is the god of everyday reality, of commerce and the market-place, and the god of the eternal who guides souls to the Underworld and to knowledge beyond death. He is the cleverest of the gods and he is their messenger and servant.

When Zeus was desperate to release his beloved Io from Argus, the monster with a hundred eyes that was guarding her, he appealed to Hermes. For 'there was no god cleverer than Hermes'. Hermes disguised himself as a shepherd, and began to play on his pipe of reeds as monotonously as he could and then to talk as drowsily as he could – to play and to talk, to talk and to play – until gradually Argus could not keep any of his hundred eyes open. Where Zeus' strength failed, Hermes' trickery won, and Argus was bored into surrender. When the two giants, Otus and Ephialtes, took young Ares their prisoner, bound him with chains of brass and shut him up in a big clay jar, it was once again Hermes who discovered the prisoner's whereabouts and managed stealthily to release him. And when Odysseus' men were

The sanctuary of Pan on the island of Thasos. Pan, the son of Hermes and Dryope, half-man, half-goat, was a rustic god, symbol of man's raw instincts, who also came to represent man uprooted in our modern world. 'Pan came out of the woods one day –
His skin and his hair and his eyes were gray,
The gray of the moss of walls were they –
And stood in the sun and looked his fill
At the wooded valley and wooded hill.'
ROBERT FROST

turned into swine by Circe, Hermes appeared in the guise of a young man and gave Odysseus the *moly*, a magic herb, to counteract Circe's deadly arts: magic pitted against magic, the magic that releases against the magic that ensnares, the enchantress turned into the enchanted.

Magic and trickery, mischief and lying, belong as naturally to Hermes' world as guiding souls to the Underworld and initiating men into the mysteries of death. Hermes is appointed messenger of the gods because he promises never to lie, but adds that 'it may be necessary for him not to tell the truth in order that he may not lie'. We cannot translate the highest mysteries of spirit and death and immortality into our three-dimensional world, Hermes is telling us, without lying. When we hold up as truth the forms of the visible world we stop ourselves from seeing the Truth that is within the formless substance out of which the forms were created. Whenever we speak of the soul, of the formless in the world of forms, we are bound to fall into error, half-truth and deception. Language and speech which, according to Plato, were invented by Hermes, belong to the world of form. 'The name Hermes has to do with speech and signifies that he is the interpreter, or messenger or thief, or liar, or bargainer; all that sort of thing has a great deal to do with language. . . . Speech signifies all things, and is always turning them round and round, and has two forms, true and false.'

Mercurial is the word that has come down to us from Hermes' Latin counterpart to indicate inconstancy and unpredictability. But something that appears erratic, fitful, whimsical and capricious from one perspective can, from Hermes' perspective, be the wisdom that cannot be captured in objective statements and concrete facts. A T-bone steak is undoubtedly less mercurial than Beethoven's last quartets, but we have denuded, not enriched, our world by this demand for the tangible and the objective. In fact almost everything that gives our world meaning and value – poetry, literature, religion and indeed modern science – is mercurial; elusive in appearance, inscrutable by reason alone, but solidly based in our imagination and experience. The god who bequeathed the word mercurial to our world is also the god of 'hermeneutics', the science of interpretation and explanation, which is a particular way to approach understanding. If true to Hermes' spirit, it brings light and clarity through the insight that sees through sudden openings in an instant – which is the elusive spirit of 'finding and thieving'.

Hermes' world is not the heroic world of objective facts and rigid absolutes but the shifting world of reality that includes endless transformations. Around Hermes' magic rod were coiled two serpents: symbols of transformation into new life. 'This is the rod of Hermes: touch what you will with it, they say, and it becomes gold. Nay, but bring what you will and I will transmute it into Good. Bring sickness, bring death, bring poverty and reproach, bring trial for life – all these things through the rod of Hermes shall be turned to profit.'

Hermes has, throughout history, been seen as the patron of alchemy – the art of the transmutation of base metals into gold, symbolic of the transformation of man through the descent of spirit. Through all our transformations Hermes hovers before us: a bridge between ourselves and what we feel greater than ourselves, between what we know and what we dimly perceive, between what we are and what we are not and yet feel called upon to become, between the last horizon of our known self and the compelling mystery which encloses it as the universe the earth. Whether the compelling mystery drives us to explore outer space or the depths of the Underworld, he is always our guide – the god of the borderlines urging us to break through established frontiers into what Plato calls 'the beyond'.

He was called the 'light bringer', but he was also the god of the night, its magic, its inventiveness and its hidden wisdom, the god who with his rod put men to sleep and sent them dreams, messages from beyond the border of our everyday reality that illuminate our experiences and bring eternity into time. Hermes' stone heaps marked boundaries; the flying god blurred their edges.

The herm, the stone pillar that was to be found in almost every courtyard of ancient Greece, symbolized the ambivalent nature of the god: it consisted of a head of Hermes and a huge erection, head and genitals represented together. The god of the solemn descent to the depths of spirit was also the god of sexuality. When the gods are called by Hephaistos to watch Ares and Aphrodite in the net he has laid to trap them, Hermes is the only god who is not caught in shame, anger or embarrassment. When Apollo, in his detached, inquiring way, asks him whether he would care, 'though held in those unyielding shackles, to lie in bed by golden Aphrodite's side', Hermes fantasizes freely and unselfconsciously in front of all the gods.

Hermes fantasizes but is never trapped. Whether in the realm of sexual fantasy or chasing the nymphs, dancing and mating with them 'in the depths of pleasant caves', Hermes is involved but never caught. The god of becoming embodies the longing in us to move beyond fantasy and beyond experience into our ever-expanding reality, always *en route*, never caught by the magic, the glamour of any stage in the journey, yet fully enjoying the scenery along the way. So, after we have laughed at his wit, been held in the grip of his drama, nourished ourselves in his wisdom, revelled in the colour and layers of his adventures, he still raises echo after echo in our minds and hearts. Which is not surprising, for the Hermes in us is as inexhaustible, as mysterious and as mercurial as life.

PAGE 198 Mosaic from a Roman villa, 2nd century A D. The flute is not only a musical instrument associated with Hermes, but part of the god's magical side. In Mozart's opera it is the magic flute that protects Tamino through the different tests of his journey, as Hermes guides and protects man in his voyage through different realms and adventures, through love, fear, pain and joy.

PAGE 199 Statue of a shepherd, Roman copy of a Hellenistic original. Hermes is the god of the solemn descent to the depths of spirit and the god of sexuality, the god of everyday reality, of shepherds and the marketplace, and the god of the eternal who guides souls to the Underworld and to knowledge beyond death.

ABOVE Statue of Hermes found at Nineveh, 1st–3rd century AD. Hermes' winged hat was one of the symbols of the god who represents motion and freedom and introduces fluidity, new beginnings and another dimension whenever things seem fixed, rigid and 'stuck'.

RIGHT Hermes, Roman copy of a Greek original, 450–400 BC. Along with our first image of Hermes as a divine child we have the view of him as an old man with a beard represented in the phallus shaped stone pillar, the 'herm'.

EPILOGUE

HALFWAY THROUGH THE WRITING OF THIS BOOK, I took a trip to Greece and found myself in a remote village in Crete. Time had indeed stopped, and looking at the rugged, almost primeval faces of the Cretan men and women, the first few lines of George William Russell's *Exiles* flooded through me:

> The gods have taken alien shapes upon them,
> Wild peasants driving swine
> In a strange country. Through the swarthy faces
> The starry faces shine.

A few days later, I had left the Greek light that dazzles and I was back under New York's grey skies, but the gods' starry faces have continued to shine – through baby faces and careworn faces, made-up faces and wrinkled faces, angry faces and happy faces.

> Under grey tattered skies they strain and reel there:
> Yet cannot all disguise
> The majesty of fallen gods, the beauty,
> The fire beneath their eyes. . . .
>
> And, to themselves unknown,
> They carry with them diadem and sceptre
> And move from throne to throne.

The ancient gods in their modern faces are now everywhere around me, which is why this book has been a kind of homecoming. The gods of my childhood no longer reveal themselves in lightning and thunder but they reveal themselves no less powerfully in myself, in my friends, in the men and women I encounter whether in the villages of Crete or the streets of New York. By learning to recognize the gods and goddesses in our midst, we add

Byron's name carved in stone near the temple of Poseidon at Sounion:
'Place me on Sunium's marbled
    steep,
Where nothing, save the waves
    and I,
May hear our mutual murmurs
    sweep;
There, swan-like, let me sing and
    die. . . .'   BYRON

to our lives a dimension of depth and significance which is sorely lacking when life is experienced as 'nothing but' a series of problems to be overcome and the people around us as 'nothing but' an aggregate of character traits, defences and responses.

In our longing to understand ourselves and our world, the gods of the past, very much alive today, can show us the way into our future. Because they are present in our darkness and our limitations, no less than in our greatness and our joy, they can teach us a deep acceptance of others and of ourselves in our totality; and acceptance, as the gods' myths tell us, is the first step on the way to change and transformation. Because they are so unique in their expression of the most basic aspects of living – in relationships, at work, in their sexuality, in their femininity or masculinity, in their inner lives – they can free us from the prevalent stereotypes of being and behaving and help us connect with our own uniqueness. Finally, because they are so natural, concrete and worldly in their divinity, they can help heal our culture's split between the earthly and the divine, the secular and the religious. In the Greek gods, the eternal and the divine are fully at home with the ephemeral and the earthly. The natural *is* the divine, and therefore nothing is accidental or meaningless. 'The singular events and their totalities reflect themselves in the eternal, and yet none of the blood and breath of living presence is lost.'

In the fourth century AD, all pagan worship was banned by a decree of Theodosius the Great. Apollo's oracle has been silenced and the paths leading to it 'are roughened by the hurrying winter rains, or tufted with green weeds'. The gods were reduced to 'phantoms of mist and cloud', 'goblin myths and hairbrain fantasies', alive only in poetic fancies and literary metaphors. But today, when our objective realities have failed us and our proud age of reason is sick unto death, there is a new readiness to welcome back the long-exiled gods and recreate for our time their richness, their power and their meaning.

'We are all under the same mental calamity', wrote Chesterton. 'We have forgotten what we really are. All that we call commonsense and rationality and practicality and positivism only means that for certain dead levels we forget that we have forgotten. All that we call spirit and art and ecstasy only means that for one awful instant we remember that we forget.' Making living, inner contact with the gods can call up the memory of our divine reality and help us to 'gather the meaning of things' and to discover in our conflicts and suffering the healing significance that leads to transformation. Apollo's oracle may have been silenced at Delphi, but the oracles inside ourselves are alive and speaking with a voice full of relevance, wisdom and wonder at the mystery of life and the miracle of man.

LEFT Herakles wrestling with the Nemean lion, Roman copy of a Hellenistic original.
'The fury of Herakles
Has swollen beyond bounds.
And now we are never out of
    danger
We have forgotten our smiles
    and our strength.'
THOMAS MERTON

PAGE 206 Basalt head of a young man, mixed Greek and Egyptian style, 1st century AD.
'And the burst of joyful
    greetings,
And the joyful dawn, were
    gone.
For the eye grows fill'd with
    gazing,
And on raptures follow
    calms. . . .'
MATTHEW ARNOLD

PAGE 207 Herakles, c. 440 BC.
'The urge, the ardour, the
    unconquerable will,
The potent, felt, interior
    command, stronger than
    words,
A message from the Heavens,
    whispering to me even in
    sleep,
These sped me on.'
WALT WHITMAN

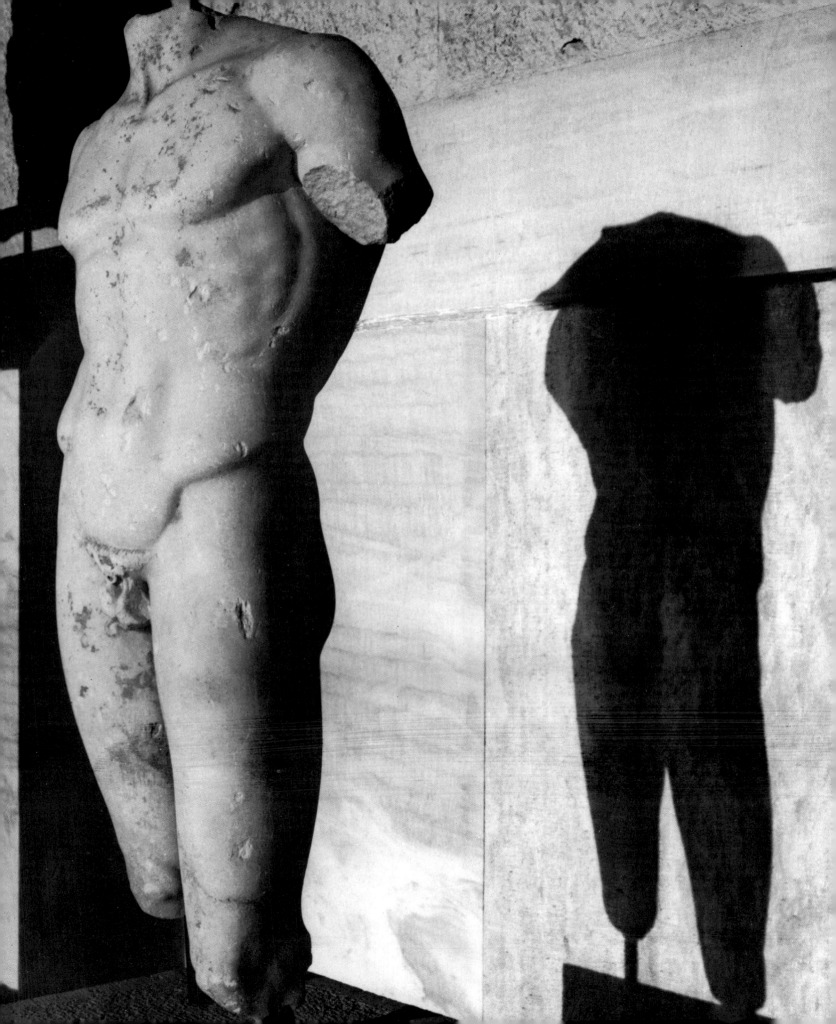

ANCIENT GREECE

THRACE

ILLYRIA

MACEDONIA

Pella ○

Therma
(Thessalonica) ○

Vergina ○

THASOS

SAMOTHRACE

MYSIA

M. Olympos ▲

LEMNOS

TROAD

Iliun (Troy) ○

EPIRUS

R. Peneus

R. Acheloos

Dodona ○

THESSALY

Pherae ○

Assos ○

KORKYRA
(CORFU)

LESBOS

PHRYGIA

THRACIAN SEA

Cape Artemision

AETOLIA

EUBOEA

LYDIA

Stratos ○

M. Parnassos ▲

Calydon ○

Delphi ○

BOEOTIA

Aulis ○

ITHACA

Thebes ○

M. Cithaeron ▲

Rhamnous ○

CHIOS

AEGEAN SEA

ACHAEA

Perachora

Eleusis ○

Ikaria ○

ELIS

M. Cyllene ▲

Corinth ○

Athens ○

SAMOS

Ephesus ○

Elis ○

ARCADIA

Nemea ○

Isthmia ○

ATTICA

Brauron ○

Olympia ○

Mycenae ○

Sounion ○

Priene ○

CARIA

Argos ○

Epidauros ○

Miletos ○

R. Alpheus

Tiryns ○

Nauplion ○

Didyma ○

Bassai ○

Tegea ○

ARGOLID

THE CYCLADES

DELOS

PELOPONNESE

MESSENIA

NAXOS

COS

SIPHNOS

CNIDOS

Sparta ○

LACONIA

MELOS

IONIAN SEA

THERA

Lindos ○

Cape Tainaron

CYTHERA

RHODES

MEDITERRANEAN
SEA

CRETE

M. Ida ▲

Knossos ○

Phaistos ○

▲ M. Dicte

Authors' Acknowledgements

There is a law as immutable as that of gravity, though not as widely proclaimed, that every author underestimates the amount of time it will take to complete a book. I have fulfilled this law with every one of my books, but this time I have decided to make it, so to speak, official, and before acknowledging all the people without whom this book would not have been possible I would like to acknowledge all the people without whom this book would have been possible in much less time. While prolonging the time it took to finish the book, they made that time, and my life, richer and, indirectly and unwittingly, they also enriched the book. On both these counts I would like to thank Nancy Nelson and the Keedick Lecture Bureau who made lecturing around the country first a part of my life and then an addiction, until writing threatened to become an activity to be indulged in the intervals from speaking; Peter Bevan who lured me away from Olympos to film a series of interviews around the country with people I had long admired and respected; Mort Janklow who, while I was working on Hermes, took me to lunch and suggested that I write a biography of Picasso, a suggestion which soon became a contract taking me away from the gods to set up the research for the Picasso project; and, finally, all my new friends who made New York feel like home within weeks of moving here from London.

Among these friends I would like to single out John Duka, Marc Leland and Mort Zuckerman who read the typescript at different stages and made many useful comments and suggestions. Tony Joseph in San Francisco and Anna Ivara in New York were invaluable both for the research they did for me on different aspects of the book and for sharing my excitement at seeing the gods gradually come alive. Nancy Gardiner and Norman Parkinson, with whom I went to Greece to try to capture the gods in modern pictures, were so totally in tune with my vision of the gods as ever-present in our lives that they became the inspiration for the God Game that we played on buses and planes around Greece to discover which blend of gods and goddesses each one of us was. Alison Mazzola and my sister, Agapi, joined in the Game as wholeheartedly as they had joined in every aspect of our Greek adventure.

Kerry Kammer, my personal assistant, gave invaluable support at every stage of the book, from his editorial help to his tireless legwork locating obscure poems and references in libraries and bookstores all over New York; Hilarie Levion typed and retyped different drafts of the book; and my mother, who had first introduced me to the gods as a child, continued to give me insights into them as a grown-up. To all of them go my deepest thanks.

To Paul Gottlieb at Abrams in New York and, especially, to Mark Boxer at Weidenfeld in London I owe a special debt for supervising with unstinting care every aspect of the book's production. I am particularly grateful to Martha Caute in London for all her editorial suggestions, for her thoroughness and for her sense of humour during our transatlantic editorial meetings. My deep thanks also go to Pat Egan in New York for her careful reading of the typescript and to Theodore Kalomirakis for capturing the book's essence in his jacket design for the American edition.

Finally I want to thank George Weidenfeld for once again setting me off on an exciting book journey, and Roloff Beny both for his masterly photographs and for his deep understanding of what was my aim from the beginning: to rediscover the ancient gods in their modern faces and recreate for our time their richness and their meaning.

ARIANNA STASSINOPOULOS

I wish to thank warmly all those who helped me when I was photographing for this book in Greece. I am particularly indebted to Dr Caroline Williams and to Dr Hector Williams, Director of the Canadian Archaeological Institute at Athens, both of whom gave me guidance in discovering remote and unusual sites. Dr Caroline Williams gave expert advice and information about the sculptures, temples and many of the other images reproduced in this book. Richard Ashton spent his holiday accompanying me to the major sites of the Peloponnese and to the important museums in Greece. Nigel Kennell assisted me on location in Athens, especially on the Acropolis. The American School of Classical Studies has given me the use of their library and generous hospitality during many trips to Greece.

Many thanks are due to Melina Mercouri, the Greek Minister of Culture, for her warm reception, and for helping me to gain easy access to many museums, especially the Agora Museum, the National Museum in Athens, and numerous small museums throughout Attica and the Peloponnese.

In Rome, the Sovrintendendenza Archeologica di Roma kindly gave me permission to photograph sculpture in the Museo Nazionale Romano (Terme Museum), some of which was under restoration, and the Capitoline Museums. I was particularly pleased to photograph some of the wonderful pieces in the 'Aeneas in Latium' exhibition, organized by Dott. ssa. Anna Sommella Mura and designed by Maurizio Di Puolo, which was held at the Antiquarium Comunale. In my own studio, I particularly want to thank Franco Bugionovi for the usual high quality in the interpretation of the black-and-white and colour images, and Antonella Carini for her collaboration in researching and preparing the material presented in this book.

In Canada, I am indebted to the Royal Ontario Museum in Toronto for their obliging co-operation and the special privileges they have afforded me. In London, the Greek and Roman departments of the British Museum allowed me to photograph special exhibits.

Finally I would like to make a tribute to the Aegean world and its gods, who have haunted and inspired me over three decades of passionate exploration.

ROLOFF BENY

Notes

Page

4 'Is he from our world?' Rainer Maria Rilke, 'Sonnets to Orpheus' in *Selected Poems of R. M. Rilke*, trans. by Robert Bly, (Harper Colophon Books, Harper and Row, New York, 1981)

7 'The fear of death'. Plato, *Apology of Socrates* in the *Dialogues*, trans. by B. Jowett (Clarendon Press, Oxford, 1871)

8 'are no longer'. James Hillman, *Re-Visioning Psychology* (Harper and Row, New York, 1975)

8 'To the imagination'. W. H. Auden, 'The Dyer's Hand' in *Collected Works* (Random House, New York, 1962)

8 'real demons to be worshipped'. R. Hinks, *Myth and Allegory in Ancient Art* (Warburg Institute, London, 1939)

9 'The faculty which'. Walter F. Otto, *The Homeric Gods*, trans. by Moses Hadas (Thames and Hudson, London, 1979)

10 'If the unconscious figures'. C. G. Jung in *The Secret of the Golden Flower: A Chinese Book of Life*, trans. by R. Wilhelm, with a commentary by C. G. Jung (Harcourt Brace Javanovich, New York, 1962)

10 'Divine Earth', *Orphic Hymn to Mother Earth* in *The Orphic Hymns*, trans. by Apostolos N. Athanassakis (Scholar Press, Missoula, Montana, 1977)

13 'First of all, Chaos'. Hesiod, *Theogony*, trans. by Norman O. Brown (The Library of Liberal Arts, The Bobbs-Merrill Co., Indianapolis, 1953)

13 'endless space of heavens'. C. G. Jung, *Memories, Dreams, Reflections* (Vintage Books, New York, 1963)

14 'One race there is'. Pindar, quoted in R. W. Livingstone, *The Greek Genius and Its Meaning to Us* (Oxford University Press, London, 1924)

14 'But as for thee, Menelaus'. Homer, *The Odyssey*, trans. by E. V. Rieu (Penguin Books, Harmondsworth, 1966)

15 'from above and through the light'. James Hillman, *The Dream and the Underworld* (Harper and Row, New York, 1979)

16 'Night gave birth'. Hesiod, op. cit.

16 'the antithetical powers'. Nikos Kazantzakis, *The Saviors of God: Spiritual Exercises* (Simon and Schuster, New York, 1960)

16 'the wounder and healer'. Karl Phillip Moritz, quoted in Karl Kerényi, *Athene, Virgin and Mother in Greek Religion*, trans. by Murray Stein (Spring Publications, Zurich, 1978)

25 'What is our duty?' Kazantzakis, op. cit.

25 'It is not a matter'. C. G. Jung, *Collected Works*, Vol. 13 (Princeton University Press, Princeton, 1953)

25 'Zeus' second consort'. Hesiod, op. cit.

26 'resolved on from untold ages'. Plato, *Epinomis* in *The Collected Dialogues*, ed. by Edith Hamilton and Huntington Cairns (Princeton University Press, Princeton, 1961)

26 'to make the web of its destiny'. Ibid.

26 'Lachesis singing the things'. Ibid.

27 'Neither, then, said I'. Plato, *The Republic* in *The Collected Dialogues*, op. cit.

27 'as the opposite'. Thomas Mann in *Mythology and Humanism, The Correspondence of Thomas Mann and Karl Kerényi*, trans. by Alexander Gelley (Cornell University Press, Ithaca and London, 1975)

27 'As metaphors speak'. Hillman, *Re-Visioning Psychology*, op. cit.

27 'We dance round'. Robert Frost, *The Secret Sits* in *The Poetry of Robert Frost*, ed. by Edward Connery Latham (Holt, Rinehart and Winston, New York, 1969, and Jonathan Cape, London, 1971). Reproduced by permission of the Estate of Robert Frost.

28 'flown out of the sorrowful'. W. K. C. Guthrie, *The Greeks and Their Gods* (Beacon Press, Boston, 1950)

28 'when a man has devoted'. Plato, 'Letter VII', quoted in *Mythology and Humanism*, op. cit.

29 'I dare do all'. William Shakespeare, *Macbeth*, *The Oxford Shakespeare* (Oxford University Press, London and New York, 1905)

29 'Man, proud man'. William Shakespeare, *Measure for Measure*, *The Oxford Shakespeare*, op. cit.

30 'The gods could not'. Hillman, *Re-Visioning Psychology*, op. cit.

30 'a momentary eternity'. Kazantzakis, op. cit.

30 'Whoever will look'. Montaigne, 'Of the Inconstancy of Our Actions', *Essays*, Vol. II (Reeves and Turner, London, 1902)

31 'But what can a man'. Jung, *Collected Works*, Vol. 11, op. cit.

31 'The morning star'. Plato, *Epinomis* in *The Collected Dialogues*, op. cit.

32 'It is *not* that astrologers'. Richard T. Tarnus, 'Uranus and Prometheus' in *Astrology Faces Mythology* (National Council for Geocosmic Research, San Francisco, 1981)

41 'Tell me is it'. Odysseus Elytis, *The Mad Pomegranate Tree* in *The Sovereign Sun*, Selected Poems by Odysseus Elytis, trans. by Kimor Friar (Temple University Press, Philadelphia, 1974)

41 'It is Herakles'. *Homeric Hymn to Herakles* in *The Homeric Hymns*, trans. by Charles Boer (Spring Publications, Irving, Texas)

42 'Equus, I love you'. Peter Shaffer, *Equus* (Avon Books, New York, 1974)

44 'Once more let it'. Rainer Maria Rilke, *Sämtliche Werke*, Vol. II, trans. by Murray Stein

46 'Why did they make'. Ernest Hemingway, *The Old Man and the Sea* (Charles Scribner's Sons, New York, 1952)

47 'The connection with'. Jung, *Collected Works*, Vol. 10, op. cit.

47 'Neither did the powerful'. *The Iliad of Homer*, trans. with an introduction by Richmond Lattimore (The University of Chicago Press, Chicago and London, 1951)

53 'I am the eye'. P. B. Shelley, *Hymn of Apollo* in *The Poetical Works of Shelley* (Oxford University Press, London, 1934)

53 'all creation's growth'. William Rose Benét, *Young Apollo* in *Starry Harness and Other Poems* (Duffield and Green, New York, 1933)

53 'I am taller'. Jean Giraudoux, *The Apollo of Bellac*, trans. by Maurice Valency (Samuel French Inc, New York, 1954)

54 'It proclaims the presence'. Otto, *The Homeric Gods*, op. cit.

54 'The tones of music'. Vincent Vycinas, *Earth and Gods* (Martinus Nijhoff, The Hague, 1969)

55 'In Apollo all the splendour'. Walter F. Otto, *Dionysus: Myth and Cult* (Spring Publications, Dallas, Texas, 1981)

57 'Did the stars'. Alfred Noyes, *The Inn of Apollo* in *Collected Poems* (John Murray, London, 1950, and J. B. Lippincott, Philadelphia, 1950)

57 'Apollo from his shrine'. John Milton, *On the Morning of Christ's Nativity* in *The English Poems of John Milton* (Oxford University Press, London, 1940)

57 'The languid strings'. William Blake, *To the Muses* in *William Blake*, introduced and ed. by J. Bronowski, (Penguin Books, London, 1958)

57 'drawing it forth'. James Hillman, *The Myth of Analysis* (Harper and Row, New York, 1978)

58 'Apollo loved her'. *Bullfinch's Mythology* (Thomas Y. Crowell, New York, 1913)

59 'When I was still'. Ovid, *Metamorphoses*, trans. by Mary M. Innes (Penguin Books, Harmondsworth, 1955)

60 'Not one touch'. John Cowper Powys, *To Apollo* in *Poems*, ed. and with an introduction by Kenneth Hopkins (Colgate University Press, Hamilton, New York, and Macdonald & Co., London, 1964). © The Estate of John Cowper Powys, 1964. Reproduced by permission of Laurence Pollinger Ltd and the Estate of John Cowper Powys.

60 'Let me compare'. Plato, *Phaedrus* in Jowett, op. cit.

64 'Or view the Lord'. Lord Byron, *Childe Harold* in *The Poetical Works of Lord Byron* (Oxford University Press, London and New York, 1945)

70 'In the figure'. Karl Kerényi, 'A Mythological Image of Girlhood' in *Facing the Gods*, ed. by James Hillman (Spring Publications, Irving, Texas, 1980)

70 'It is the crystal-clear'. Otto, *The Homeric Gods*, op. cit.

72 'I was led by the willow'. Benét, *Ghost Actaeon* in *Starry Harness and Other Poems*, op. cit.

72 'must kill him'. Hillman, *Re-Visioning Psychology*, op. cit.
73 'If you will contemplate'. C.G.Jung, *Mysterium Coniunctionis* (Princeton University Press, Princeton, 1963)
75 'Some fiercer caring'. May Sarton, *Journal of a Solitude* (W.W.Norton, New York, 1938)
75 'Ask her who means'. Hermann Hesse, *My Belief*, trans. by Denren Lindley (Jonathan Cape, London, 1976)
75 'Niobe, she of the'. *The Iliad of Homer*, trans. by Lattimore, op. cit.
75 'And when she has'. *Homeric Hymn to Artemis* in *The Homeric Hymns*, op. cit.
78 'a close god'. Michael P.Sipiora, 'A Soul's Journey: Albert Camus, Tuberculosis, and Aphrodite', *Spring 1981* (Spring Publications, Dallas, Texas, 1981)
78 'She even leads'. *Homeric Hymn to Aphrodite* in *The Homeric Hymns*, op. cit.
78 'Earth's archetypal Eve'. Wilfrid Scawen Blunt, *The Venus of Milo* in *The Love Sonnets of Proteus* (Kegan Paul, Trench, Trubner and Co. Ltd, London, 1898)
80 'No one, I think'. Plato, *Symposium* in *The Collected Dialogues*, op. cit.
80 'Perhaps no religion'. Kenneth Clark, *The Nude* (Pantheon, New York, 1956)
80 'And the Hours'. *The Second Homeric Hymn to Aphrodite* in *The Homeric Hymns*, op. cit.
81 'her white cold fire'. D.H.Lawrence, *Twilight in Italy* (Penguin Books, London, 1960)
81 'Only Venus comes'. Marsilio Ficino, *The Book of Life*, trans. by Charles Boer (Spring Publications, Irving, Texas, 1979)
81 'Do not imagine'. W.H.Auden, *Venus Will Now Say a Few Words* in *Collected Poems* (Faber, London, and Random House, New York, 1976)
81 'Great is my power'. Euripides, *Hippolytus*, trans. by Moses Hadas and John McLean (Bantam Books, New York, 1960)
83 'With one sharp-taken'. Rupert Brooke, *The Goddess in the Wood* in *Rupert Brooke's Poems* (Folio Society, London, 1948)
83 'Torches are made'. William Shakespeare, *Venus and Adonis*, *The Oxford Shakespeare*, op. cit.
83 'When Pygmalion returned'. Ovid, op. cit.
85 'If the all too obvious'. Alexander Solzhenitsyn, 'Nobel Lecture' (Ad Hoc Committee for Intellectual Freedom, 1973)

85 'She who awakens'. *Homeric Hymn to Aphrodite* in *The Homeric Hymns*, op. cit.
85 'Yet whatso'er of good'. W.S.Blunt, op. cit.
88 'And after strain'. W.H.Auden, *Venus Will Now Say a Few Words*, op. cit.
88 'Embracing her'. Simone de Beauvoir, *The Second Sex* (Jonathan Cape, London, 1953)
88 'In the blessed'. Angelos Sikelianos, *Aphrodite Rising* in *Angelos Sikelianos: Selected Poems*, trans. and introduced by Edmund Keeley and Philip Sherrard (Princeton University Press, Princeton, 1979). Copyright © 1979 by Edmund Keeley and Philip Sherrard. Reprinted by permission of Princeton University Press.
97 'Pour Bacchus'. Ralph Waldo Emerson, *Bacchus* in *Masterpieces of American Poets*, ed. by Mark van Doren (Garden City Publishing, New York, 1936)
99 'This new divinity'. Euripides, *The Bacchants*, trans. by Moses Hadas and John McLean (Bantam Books, New York, 1960)
99 'When I remember'. *Homeric Hymn to Dionysos* in *The Homeric Hymns*, op. cit.
100 'The world man knows'. Walter F.Otto, *Dionysos: Myth and Cult* (Spring Publications, Dallas, Texas, 1981)
100 'the power to free'. Ibid.
100 'In the first place'. Plato, *Laws* in *The Collected Dialogues*, op. cit.
100 'The praise of Bacchus'. John Dryden, *Alexander's Feast* in *The Poems of John Dryden* (Oxford University Press, London and New York, 1910)
104 'When your body is spinning'. Reshad Field, *The Last Barrier* (Harper and Row, New York, 1976)
105 'As the worshipping Corybantes'. Plato, *Ion* in *The Collected Dialogues*, op. cit.
105 'This madness'. Otto, *Dionysos: Myth and Cult*, op. cit.
106 'They gird themselves'. Ibid.
106 'the unutterable could'. Bennett Simon, *Mind and Madness in Ancient Greece: The Classic Roots of Modern Psychiatry* (Cornell University Press, Ithaca, New York, 1978)
107 'the final secrets'. Otto, *Dionysos: Myth and Cult*, op. cit.
108 'At times we are pulled'. Christine Downing, 'Ariadne: Mistress of the Labyrinth' in *Facing The Gods*, op. cit.
109 'I have instituted my dances'. Euripides, *The Bacchants*, op. cit.

109 'the theatre of mythology'. Kerényi, *Athene, Virgin and Mother in Greek Religion*, op. cit.
115 'Your fine sons'. Hesiod, op. cit.
115 'Son of Cronos'. Ibid.
115 'Hail, O Zeus'. Cleanthes, *Hymn to Zeus* in *The Penguin Book of Greek Verse*, introduced and ed. by Constantine A. Trypanis (Penguin Books, Harmondsworth, 1971). Copyright © Constantine A. Trypanis, 1971. Reprinted by permission of Penguin Books.
116 'Zeus is the first'. *The Orphic Hymns*, op. cit.
120 'Ageless, lusty'. Graham Hough, *The Children of Zeus* in *Legends and Pastorals, Poems* by Graham Hough (Duckworth, London, 1961)
120 'A sudden blow'. W.B.Yeats, *Leda and the Swan* in *The Collected Poems of W.B.Yeats* (Macmillan, London and New York, 1950). Reproduced by permission of Michael B.Yeats, Anne Yeats and Macmillan London Ltd and Macmillan New York Inc.
120 'Father ... do not stop'. Angelos Sikelianos, *Daedalus* in *Selected Poems*, op. cit.
120 'Now I am also'. Rainer Maria Rilke, *Evening in Skåne* in *Selected Poems*, op. cit.
129 'So speaking'. *The Iliad of Homer*, trans. by Lattimore, op. cit.
129 'fully met, matched'. Christine Downing, *The Goddess, Mythological Images of the Feminine* (Crossroad, New York, 1981)
129 'Stone, steel, dominions'. A.E.Housman, XXIV in *More Poems* in *A.E.Housman: Collected Poems* (Penguin Books, Harmondsworth, 1956)
129 'The sun, the child'. Stesichorus, in *The Penguin Book of Greek Poetry*, op. cit.
131 'Or else flush'd Ganymede'. Alfred, Lord Tennyson, *The Palace of Art* in *Tennyson: Poems and Plays* (Oxford University Press, Oxford and London, 1965)
134 'High Zeus'. *The Iliad of Homer*, trans. by Lattimore, op. cit.
138 'by the artifice'. *The Odes of Pindar*, trans. by Richmond Lattimore (University of Chicago Press, Chicago, 1947)
138 'I'll start this singing'. *Homeric Hymn to Athena* in *The Homeric Hymns*, op. cit.
138 'The Man is the source'. Aeschylus, *The Eumenides*, trans. by Robert Sagles (Penguin Books, London, 1966)

138 'She threw round'. Homer, *The Iliad*, trans. by E.V.Rieu (Penguin Books, Harmondsworth, 1950)
140 'Cities are the gift'. Lewis Richard Farnell, *The Cult of the Greek States*, Vol. I (Aegean Press, Chicago, 1971)
140 'Inclusion of the'. James Hillman, 'On the Necessity of Abnormal Psychology: Ananke and Athene' in *Facing the Gods*, op. cit.
141 'the nearness of the divine'. Otto, *The Homeric Gods*, op. cit.
141 'But why we should'. W.H.Auden, *Ode to Gaea*, in *W.H.Auden: Collected Poems*, op. cit.
142 'associated with winged'. Downing, op. cit.
145 'Athena was all'. Ibid.
145 'I turned your face'. May Sarton, *The Muse as Medusa* in *Collected Poems* (W.W.Norton, New York, 1974)
147 'Homer meant by Athena'. Plato, *Cratylus*, in *The Collected Dialogues*, op. cit.
151 'Goddess of Wisdom!' Lord Byron, *Childe Harold* in *The Poetical Works of Byron*, op. cit.
151 'And I in the trials'. Aeschylus, *Eumenides*, op. cit.
152 'Muse, sing Hermes'. *Homeric Hymn to Hermes* in *The Homeric Hymns*, op. cit.
152 'A motion and a spirit'. William Wordsworth, *Lines composed a few miles above Tintern Abbey* in *Wordsworth: Poetical Works*, ed. by T.Hutchinson (Oxford University Press, London and New York, 1969)
161 'This relativity craze'. Thomas Merton, *Space Song* in *The Collected Poems of Thomas Merton* (New Directions, New York, 1977, and Sheldon Press, London, 1978)
162 'Perhaps Hera had only'. Downing, *The Goddess, Mythological Images of the Feminine*, op. cit.
164 'Hera is not'. Ibid.
164 'Here I sing'. *Homeric Hymn to Hera* in *The Homeric Hymns*, op. cit.
168 'The continuous fire'. Georges Dumezil, *Archaic Roman Religion* (University of Chicago Press, Chicago, 1966)
168 'the almost irresistible'. Jung, *Collected Works*, Vol. 9. op. cit.
169 'She sees all things'. *Ovid's Fasti*, trans. by Sir James Frazer (Harvard University Press, Cambridge)
169 'the builder of the house'. Barbara Kirksey, 'Hestia: A Background of Psychological Focusing' in *Facing the Gods*, op. cit.

169 'Now even as the mind'. Plato, *Phaedrus* in *The Collected Dialogues*, op. cit.

170 'Lord Ares'. *The Orphic Hymns*, op. cit.

170 'Ares, lord of strife'. Aeschylus, *Agamemnon*, trans. by E. D. A. Morshead in *Seven Famous Greek Plays*, ed. with introductions by Whitney J. Oates and Eugene O'Neill Jr. (The Modern Library, Random House, New York, 1938, 1950)

175 'Sing, clear-voiced Muse'. *Homeric Hymn to Hephaistos* in *Hesiod, The Homeric Hymns and Homerica*, trans. by H. G. Evelyn-White (Loeb Classical Library, Heinemann, London, 1914)

176 'When he heard'. Homer, *The Odyssey*, trans. by E. V. Rieu (Penguin Books, Harmondsworth, 1966)

177 'nothing better'. Ibid.

177 'His shouts brought'. Ibid.

178 'Every mother'. C. G. Jung, 'The Psychological Aspects of the Kore', in *Essays on a Science of Mythology* (Princeton University Press, Princeton, 1969)

178 'And forth again'. Alfred, Lord Tennyson, *Demeter and Persephone* in *Tennyson: Poems and Plays*, op. cit.

178 'Demeter and Kore'. Jung, 'The Psychological Aspects of the Kore', op. cit.

180 'Then I, Earth-Goddess'. Tennyson, *Demeter and Persephone*, op. cit.

183 'Persephone returns'. Charlene Spretnak, *Lost Goddesses of Early Greece* (Beacon Press, Boston, 1978)

183 'Verily I say unto you'. St John 12:26

183 'and bless'. Tennyson, *Demeter and Persephone*, op. cit.

184 'a seed in each'. Patricia Berry, 'The Rape of Demeter, Persephone and Neurosis', *Spring 1975* (Spring Publications, New York, 1975)

185 'It is as if the virgin'. Gail Thomas, 'Afterword' in *Images of the Untouched*, ed. by Joanne Stroud and Gail Thomas (Spring Publications, Texas, 1982)

185 'and her look'. Sikelianos, *Thalero* in *Selected Poems*, op. cit.

187 'practise death'. Plato, *Phaedo* in *The Collected Dialogues*, op. cit.

187 'All descents'. Sylvia Brinton Perera, *Descent to the Goddess* (Inner City Books, Toronto, 1981)

187 'They are the souls'. Virgil, *The Aeneid*, Book VI

188 'a slow decaying'. Perera, op. cit.

188 'Life becomes'. Hillman, *Re-Visioning Psychology*, op. cit.

193 'Born in the morning'. *Homeric Hymn to Hermes* in *The Homeric Hymns*, op. cit.

193 'Few of us automatically'. William G. Doty, 'Hermes' Heteronymous Appellations' in *Facing The Gods*, op. cit.

194 'there was no god'. Edith Hamilton, *Mythology, Timeless Tales of Gods and Heroes* (New American Library, New York, 1953)

194 'Pan came out of the woods'. Frost, *Pan with Us* in *The Poetry of Robert Frost*, op. cit.

196 'it may be necessary'. David L. Miller, *The New Polytheism* (Spring Publications, Dallas, Texas, 1981)

196 'The name Hermes'. Plato, *Cratylus* in *The Collected Dialogues*, op. cit.

196 'This is the rod'. Arrian, *The Discourses of Epictetus* (Macmillan, London, 1925)

203 'The gods have taken'. George William Russell, *Exiles* in *Voices of the Stones* (Macmillan, London, 1925). Reproduced by permission of Colin Smythe Limited on behalf of the AE Estate

203 'Under grey tattered'. Ibid.

203 'Place me on Sunium's'. Lord Byron, *Don Juan* in *The Poetical Works of Lord Byron*, op. cit.

205 'The singular events'. Otto, *The Homeric Gods*, op. cit.

205 'are roughened'. George Savage-Armstrong, *The Closing of the Oracle* in *A Garland from Greece* (Longmans, London, 1882)

205 'phantoms of mist'. Ibid.

205 'goblin myths'. Ibid.

205 'We are all under'. G. K. Chesterton, 'The Ethics of Elfland' in *G. K. Chesterton*, selected by W. H. Auden (Faber, London, 1970)

205 'The fury of Herakles'. Merton, *Untitled* in *The Collected Poems of Thomas Merton*, op. cit.

205 'And the burst of joyful'. Matthew Arnold, *The New Sirens* in *Arnold: Poetical Works*, ed. by C. B. Tinker and H. F. Lowry (Oxford University Press, London and New York, 1950)

205 'The urge, the ardour'. Walt Whitman, *Prayer of Columbus* in *Leaves of Grass*, ed. by Harold W. Blodgett and Scully Bradley (New York University Press, New York, and University of London Press, London, 1965)

List of Illustrations

page numbers in *italic* indicate pages on which colour plates appear

Page

1 Detail of a marble grave stele from the Dipylon area, *c.* 560 BC. National Museum, Athens

2 Portion of an Archaic grave stele from Laurion in Attica, *c.* 500 BC. National Museum, Athens

6 Detail of funerary mask from Mycenae, gold, 16th century BC. National Museum, Athens

11 Archaic goddess of fertility suckling twins, produced by Greeks living in Megara Hyblaea, limestone, 540–530 BC. National Archaeological Museum, Syracuse

17 Detail of a statue of a youth found at Lavinium in southern Italy, terracotta, 4th–3rd centuries BC. Campidoglio Museum, Rome

18 Detail of the 'Mourning Athena', marble relief, *c.* 450 BC. Acropolis Museum, Athens

19 Winged Nike fastening her sandal, from the frieze of the temple of Athena Nike, Athens, marble, *c.* 410 BC. Acropolis Museum, Athens

20 Kore, marble, *c.* 520 BC. Acropolis Museum, Athens

21 Detail of the Calf-bearer, marble, *c.* 570 BC. Acropolis Museum, Athens

22 Lapith woman from the west pediment of the temple of Zeus at Olympia, marble, *c.* 460 BC. Olympia Museum

23 Apollo from the west pediment of the temple of Zeus at Olympia, marble, *c.* 460 BC. Olympia Museum

24 The 'Asklepios of Mounychia', found in Piraeus, marble, probably Hellenistic of the 2nd century BC. National Museum, Athens

33 Acanthus, with the Hephaisteion in Athens in the background

34 Lilies

35 Asphodel

36 Wild narcissi

37 Poppies and wheat

38 Olive tree

39 Pomegranate

40 Temple of Herakles at Agrigento in Sicily, end of the 6th century BC

43 Statue of Poseidon, found at Cherchel (ancient Iol), Roman copy in marble of a Greek bronze. Museum of Antiquities, Algiers

44–5 Slab from the eastern frieze of the Parthenon showing Poseidon, Apollo and Artemis, marble, *c.* 442–438 BC. Acropolis Museum, Athens

48 Head of a statue thought to represent Poseidon found in the sea off Cape Artemision, bronze, *c.* 460 BC. National Museum, Athens

49 Mt Phengari, Samothrace

50 Octopuses drying in the sun at Nauplion

51 Triton from the central panel of a floor mosaic from Magoula, near Sparta, end of 3rd–beginning of 2nd century AD. Sparta Museum

52 'Apollo of the Tiber River', Roman copy of a Greek original of the 5th century BC. Terme Museum, Rome

56 The Muse, marble, Roman copy of a Greek original of the first half of the 2nd century BC. Campidoglio Museum, Rome

60 Head of Apollo on a silver tetradrachm of the Chalcidian League, 392–358 BC. Royal Ontario Museum, Toronto (Museum photo)

61 Archaic temple of Apollo at Corinth, mid 6th century BC

62 Theatre at Delphi with the temple of Apollo beyond, 4th century BC

63 Detail of the Charioteer, bronze, *c.* 488 BC. Delphi Museum

64 Temple of Apollo at Didyma in Turkey, 4th century BC onwards

65 Terrace of the lions on Delos, marble, 7th century BC

66 Apollo, or possibly Eros, Roman copy of a Greek original, probably in bronze, of the 4th century BC. Terme Museum, Rome

67 Apollo, Roman copy in marble of a Greek bronze of the mid 5th century BC. Cherchel Museum, Algeria

68 Artemis and Apollo from the north frieze of the Siphnian Treasury, marble, *c.* 525 BC. Delphi Museum

71 Ephesian Artemis amongst other museum pieces at Ephesus, marble, probably Roman. Ephesus Museum

74 Dying Niobid, marble, *c.* 450–440 BC. Terme Museum, Rome

76 Detail of a statue of Artemis, Roman copy in marble of a Greek bronze of the 5th century BC. Corinth Museum

77 Detail of a statue of Artemis, Roman copy in marble of a Greek original found at Aulis at the end of the 5th century BC. Thebes Museum

79 Statue of Aphrodite from Cyrene in Libya, marble, Roman copy of a Hellenistic original, *c.* 100 BC. Terme Museum, Rome

84 Head of Aphrodite, terracotta, *c.* 300 BC. Corinth Museum

86 Torso of, probably, Eros, marble, Roman copy of a Greek original of the 5th century BC. Sparta Museum

87 Detail of the 'Esquiline Venus', marble, end of 1st century BC – beginning of 1st century AD (Augustinian period). Palazzo dei Conservatori, Rome

88 Aphrodite from the east pediment of the Parthenon, marble, *c.* 437–432 BC. British Museum

89 Aphrodite emerging from the sea, Roman copy of a Greek original of the 4th century BC or later. Archaeological Museum, Seville

90 Aphrodite emerging from the sea on the central panel of the Ludovisi Throne, marble, *c.* 460 BC. Terme Museum, Rome

91 Flute player on a side panel of the Ludovisi Throne, marble, *c.* 460 BC. Terme Museum, Rome

92 Relief of Zeus on a rectangular base, 1st century AD. Corinth Museum

93 Relief of Demeter on a rectangular base, 1st century AD. Corinth Museum

94 Dionysos riding a panther, pebble mosaic from the House of the Lion Hunt at Pella in Macedonia, end of the 4th century BC. Pella, Macedonia

95 Dionysos and Ariadne on the bronze crater of Derveni, *c.* 300 BC. Archaeological Museum, Thessalonica

96 Head of Dionysos from a Roman villa at Corinth, mosaic, probably 2nd century AD. Corinth Museum

98 Dionysos on a marble crater found near Sparta, 2nd century AD. Sparta Museum

101 Theatre of Dionysos in Athens, *c.* 342–326 BC

102 Detail of a statue of Dionysos, Roman copy of a Greek original of the 4th century BC. Terme Museum, Rome

103 Dionysos and a young satyr on the lid of a bronze vessel, *c.* 300 BC. Archaeological Museum, Praenesto

104 Head of Dionysos on a silver tetradrachm of Naxos, 430–420 BC. Royal Ontario Museum, Toronto (Museum photo)

105 Reverse of the coin above showing Silenus, 430–420 BC. Royal Ontario Museum, Toronto (Museum photo)

109 Dionysos from the east pediment of the Parthenon, marble, *c.* 437–432 BC. British Museum

110 Vine-growing, mosaic, Roman. Cherchel Museum, Algeria

111 Sanctuary of Dionysos at Ikaria in Attica

112 Dancing girl on a plaque found in the theatre of Dionysos in Athens, Roman copy of a Greek original of 350–300 BC. National Museum, Athens

113 Theatre at Side in Turkey, 2nd century AD

114 Zeus, marble, Roman copy of a Greek original of the 5th century BC. Royal Ontario Museum, Toronto (Museum photo)

117 Temple of Zeus, Athens, 6th century BC–2nd century AD

118–19 Mt Dicte, Crete

121 Mt Olympos

122 Temple of Zeus at Nemea, 4th century BC

123 Clouds and sky

124 Temple of Hera at Paestum in southern Italy, mid 6th century BC and later

125 Temple of Zeus in Athens, 6th century BC–2nd century AD

126 Column drums from the temple of Zeus at Olympia, 468 BC

127 Sanctuary of Hera near Argos. In the centre are the ruins of the New Temple, *c.* 420–410 BC

128 Sunset at Santorini

130 Statue of Castor in front of the proscenium of the Roman theatre at Lepcis Magna (modern Labdah), Libya, marble, Roman

131 Zeus on a silver coin of Alexander the Great, 324 BC. Royal Ontario Museum, Toronto (Museum photo)

132 Detail of a statue of Zeus and Ganymede, terracotta, 500–475 BC. Olympia Museum
133 Ganymede and the eagle, marble, 2nd century AD. Terme Museum, Rome
134 Temple of Zeus at Stratos, Acarnania, 4th century BC
135 Theatre at Dodona, c. 300 BC
136 Deidamia being abducted by the Centaur Eurytion from the west pediment of the temple of Zeus at Olympia, c. 460 BC. Olympia Museum
137 Lapith and Centaur fighting, detail of a metope from the south face of the Parthenon, marble, c. 448–442 BC. British Museum
139 Head of a statue of Athena found at Piraeus in 1959, bronze, mid 4th century BC. National Museum, Athens
143 Remains of the Archaic temple of Athena at Assos in the Troad, Turkey, c. 530 BC
144 Head of a Gorgon on the breast of the Kistophoros Caryatid from the Lesser Propylaea at Eleusis, marble, c. 30–25 BC. Eleusis Museum
146 Detail of an Archaistic statue of Athena, marble, Roman. Corinth Museum
147 Head of Athena, clay, 490 BC. Olympia Museum
148 Statue of Athena, perhaps a local product of Lavinium in southern Italy where it was found, terracotta, possibly dating from the 5th century BC. Campidoglio Museum, Rome
149 Statue of Athena from the Old Temple on the Acropolis, Athens, marble, as it was renovated by Peisistratos in 525 BC. Acropolis Museum, Athens
150 View of the Erechtheion and the Caryatid Porch, c. 410 BC
151 View of the Erechtheion, c. 410 BC
152 Parthenon sculpture in storage
153 Mt Cyllene
154 Parthenon, third quarter of the 5th century BC
155 Temple of Athena Nike, on the Acropolis in Athens, late 5th century BC
156 Tholos at Delphi, 4th century BC
157 Temple of Apollo at Bassai, late 5th century BC
158 Sea
159 Temple of Poseidon at Sounion, mid 5th century BC
160 View of Lake Vouliagmene from Perachora

163 So-called head of Hera, recently identified as the head of the Sphinx, found in the sanctuary of Hera at Olympia, limestone, c. 590 BC. Olympia Museum
165 View from the fortress of Palamidi at Nauplion looking towards the mountains of the eastern Peloponnese
166 Temple of Hera at Olympia, early 6th century BC
167 Typhon, from the Archaic temple of Athena on the Acropolis at Athens, limestone, c. 570 BC. Acropolis Museum, Athens
171 Detail of a statue of a Spartan warrior, once thought to represent Leonidas, marble, 490–480 BC. Sparta Museum
173 Ares fighting the giants, from the north frieze of the Siphnian Treasury, marble, c. 525 BC. Delphi Museum
174 View from the temple of Hephaistos looking towards the Acropolis in Athens, c. 450–440 BC
179 Demeter, Triptolemus and Kore, relief from Eleusis, marble, c. 440–430 BC. National Museum, Athens
180 Shrine of the Great Gods on Samothrace, 4th–3rd centuries BC
182 Kistophoros Caryatid, marble, c. 30–25 BC. Eleusis Museum
184 Ear of wheat on a silver stater of Metapontum, 550–480 BC. Royal Ontario Museum, Toronto (Museum photo)
185 Head of Persephone on a silver dekadrachm of Syracuse, 415–357 BC, Royal Ontario Museum, Toronto (Museum photo)
186 Detail of a funerary lekythos, c. 420 BC. National Museum, Athens
189 Head of the 'Volomandra kouros', a funerary kouros from Volomandra in Attica, marble, 550–540 BC. National Museum, Athens
191 Detail of the statue of Hermes and Dionysos, thought to be by Praxiteles, marble, c. 350–340 BC. Olympia Museum
192 Palestra at Olympia, 3rd century BC
195 Sanctuary of Pan, Thasos
198 Pastoral scene on a mosaic from a Roman villa, 2nd century AD. Corinth Museum
199 Statue of shepherd, marble, Roman copy of a Hellenistic original, probably of the 2nd century BC. Cherchel Museum, Algeria

200 Detail of a statue of Hermes found at Nineveh, limestone with inlaid eyes, 1st–early 3rd century AD. Iraq Museum, Baghdad
201 Hermes in the form of a herm, Roman copy of the Alkamenes type of 450–400 BC. Piraeus Museum
202 Byron's signature near the temple of Poseidon at Sounion
204 Herakles strangling the Nemean lion, marble, Roman copy of a Hellenistic group. Isthmia Museum
206 Head of a young man in mixed Greek and Egyptian style from Alexandria, basalt, 1st century AD. British Museum
207 Torso of, possibly, Herakles, found in the Athenian Agora, marble, c. 440 BC. Stoa of Attalos, Athens

Index

Numbers in *italic* refer to illustrations

ACHILLES, 14, 134, 141, 175
Actaeon, 70, 72
Admetus, King, 60
Adonis, 82, 83
Aeneas, 12, 59, 188
Aeschylus, 8, 12, 15, 25, 59, 80, 100, 116, 120, 138, 140, 141, 151, 170
Agamemnon, 59, 141, 175
Agrigento, *40*
Albee, Edward, 161
Alcinous, King, 177
Alcmena, 41, 120, 162
Amazons, 131
Amphitryon, 120
Anchises, 80
Andromeda, 46
Aphrodite (Venus), 8, 12, 13, 14, 25, 31, 32, 70, 75, 78–85, *79, 81, 84, 87, 88, 89, 90*, 164, 172, 176, 177, 197
Apollo, 12, 14, 23, 25, 27, *44–5, 52*, 53–60, *60, 64, 66, 67, 68*, 69, 74, 85, 116, 131, 138, 140, 152, 172, 175, 177, 193, 197, 205
Arachne, 142, 145
Ares (Mars), 8, 13, 14, 25, 31, 32, 129, 142, 170–3, *173*, 176, 177, 194, 196, 197
Argonauts, 131
Ariadne, *95*, 107–8
Aristophanes, 100
Aristotle, 8, 13, 28, 32, 107
Arnold, Matthew, quoted, 205
Arrian, quoted, 196–7
Artemis (Diana), 14, 16, 25, *44–5*, 55, 64, *68*, 69–75, *71, 76, 77*, 116, 175
Asklepios, *24*
Assos, *143*
Asteria, 120
Athena (Minerva), 9, 14, *18, 20, 21*, 25, *33, 38*, 131, 138–45, *139, 142*, 146, 147, 148, 149, 170, 172, 175, 177
Athens:
  Acropolis, 8–9, *38*; Erechtheion, *150, 151*; Parthenon, *154*; temple of Athena Nike, *155*; temple of Hephaistos, *33, 174*; temple of Zeus, *117, 125*; theatre of Dionysos, *101, 112*
Atropus, 26
Auden, W.H., quoted, 8, 81, 88, 141

BACCHUS *see* Dionysos
Bacchylides, quoted, 16
Bassai, *157*
Beauvoir, Simone de, quoted, 88
Bellerophon, 131
Benét, William Rose, quoted, 53, 70, 72

Blake, William, 26
  quoted, 57
Blunt, Wilfrid Scawen, quoted, 78, 85
Brooke, Rupert, quoted, 83
Byblos, 81
Byron, Lord, quoted, 53, 64, 151, 203

CADMUS, King, 70
Callinos, 26
Calliope, 55
Calypso, 46, 81
Campbell, Joseph, quoted, 26
Cassandra, 58–9, *59*
Cassiopeia, Queen, 46
Castor, *130*
Centaurs, 100, *136, 137*
Chesterton, G.K., quoted, 205
Chthonic deities, 14, 15
Circe, 81, 196
Clark, Kenneth, quoted, 80
Cleanthes, quoted, 115
Cleopatra, 81
Clio, 55
Clotho, 25, 26
Clytemnestra, 59
Corinth, *61*, 81
Crete, 7, 108, *118*, 203
Cronos, 31, 80, 115, 116, 129, 168
Cyclopes, 46, 60, 115, 116
Cymothoe, 88

DAEDALUS, 120
Danaë, 120
Daphne, 57–8, *59*
Daphnis, 81
Deidamia, *136*
Deimos, 172
Delos, *65*, 69
Delphi, 12, 27, 55, 60, *62*, 168, *156*, 205
Demeter, 8, 14, 15, 16, *37, 93*, 175, 178–85, *179*
Demodocus, 177
Descartes, René, 57
Dido, 12
Didyma, *64*
Diomedes, 170
Dione, 88
Dionysos (Bacchus), 12, 14, 55, 57, 59, 60, *62*, 85, *94, 95, 96*, 97–112, *98, 102, 103, 104, 109*, 129, 176, 188, *191*
Dodona, *135*
Dolon, 141
Downing, Christine, quoted, 108, 129, 142, 145, 162, 164
Dryden, John, quoted, 100
Dryope, 194
Dumezil, Georges, quoted, 168

ECHO, 162
Einstein, Albert, 194
Eleusinian Mysteries, 15, 28, 183, 184
Eleusis, 183, 184
Eliot, T.S., 72
Elysian Fields, 14
Elytis, Odysseus, quoted, 41
Emerson, R.W., quoted, 97
Empedocles, 28
Ephesus, 70, 73
Ephialtes, 194
Erato, 57
Erichthonios, 177
Erinyes, 25
Eros, 13, *66*, 78, 80, 85, *86*, 172, 173
Euripides, 12, 26, 29, 60, 81–2, 97, 99, 106, 109, 162
Europa, 120
Eurynome, 116
Eurytion, *136*
Euterpe, 57

FARNELL, Lewis Richard, quoted, 140
Fates, 25–6
Ficino, Marsilio, quoted, 81
Field, Reshad, quoted, 104–5
Freud, Sigmund, 31, 81, 97
Frost, Robert, quoted, 27, 194
Furies, 25, 141, 145

GAIA, 14, 115, 141, 177, 180, 181, 183
Gandhi, Mahatma, quoted, 173
Ganymede, *132, 133*
Giraudoux, Jean, quoted, 53–4
Glauce, 88
Goethe, Johann, 28
Gorgon, *144*, 145, *148*
Graces, the three, 116
Guthrie, W.K.C., quoted, 28

HADES (Pluto), 14, 15, 107, 178, 181, 183, 187–8
Harmonia, 172, 173
Hecate, 181
Helen, 32
Helios, 181
Hemingway, Ernest, quoted, 46
Hephaistos (Vulcan), 14, 32, 75, 129, 138, 162, 175–7, 197
Hera (Juno), 8, 12, 14, 16, *34*, 83, 120, 129, 140, 161–4, *163*, 164, 172, 176
Herakles, 9, 41, 46, 141, 162, 188, *204, 207*
Herder, Johann, quoted, 30
Hermes (Mercury), 14, 15–16, 31, 32, 141, *153*, 177, 183, 190–7, *191, 200, 201*

Hermetica, 13, 16
Herodotus, quoted, 13
Hesiod, 13, 16, 25–6, 97, 120, 168
  quoted, 16, 88, 115
Hesione, 46
Hesse, Hermann, quoted, 75
Hestia, 14, 168–9
Hillman, James, quoted, 8, 15, 27, 30, 57, 72, 140–41, 188
Hinks, R., quoted, 8–9
Hippolytus, 81–2
Homer, 13, 14, 16, 26, 28, 97, 108, 131, 147, 161, 168, 187
  Iliad, 26, 32, 47, 75, 118, 129, 134, 138, 141, 170, 177
  Odyssey, 9, 14–15, 35, 43, 175, 176–7, 193
Homeric Hymns, 41, 75, 78, 80, 85, 99–100, 138, 152, 164, 168, 175, 178, 193
Hough, Graham, quoted, 120
Hours, 25
Housman, A.E., quoted, 129
Hundred-armed Giants, 115
Hymettus, 85
Hyperion, 129

IBSEN, Henrik, 145
Ikaria, *111*
Ikarios, 109
Io, 162, 194
Iris, 183
Isa Upanishad, 161
Ithaca, 47

JAMES, William, quoted, 109
Jason, 141
Joyce, James, 161
Jung, C.G., 97, 185
  quoted, 10, 13, 25, 30, 31, 47, 73, 168, 178
Juno *see* Hera
Jupiter *see* Zeus

KAZANTZAKIS, Nikos, quoted, 16, 25, 29, 30, 99
Kerényi, Karl, quoted, 70, 85, 109
Kirksey, Barbara, quoted, 169
Kore *see* Persephone

LACHESIS, 25–6
Lapiths, *22*, 25, *137*
Lawrence, D.H., quoted, 81
Leda, 120, 131
Lethe, 28, 187
Leto, 55, 69, 74, 116
Livy, quoted, 120

MAENADS, 12, 55, 104
Maia, 190, 193
Mann, Thomas, quoted, 27

INDEX

Mars *see* Ares
Medusa, 142, 145
Melpomene, 55
Menelaus, 14–15
Mercury *see* Hermes
Merton, Thomas, quoted, 161, 205
Metis, 142, 145
Miletos, 64
Milton, John, quoted, 57
Minerva *see* Athena
Minos, King, 108
Minotaur, 108
Mnemosyne, 55, 116
Montaigne, 30
Moritz, K.P., quoted, 16
Mt Cithaeron, 162
Mt Cyllene, *153*
Mt Dicte, *118*
Mt Etna, 164
Mt Ida, 129
Mt Olympos, 14, 26, 80, *121*, 129, 131, 140, 164, 176, 183, 194
Mt Phengari, *49*
Muses, 55, *56*, 57, 85, 116
Mycenae, 7, 59

Narcissus, *36*
Nauplion, 164
Nausicaa, 46
Naxos, 108
Nemea, *122*
Neptune *see* Poseidon
Nietzsche, F., 97
Nike, *19*
Nin, Anaïs, quoted, 140
Niobe, 75
Noyes, Alfred, quoted, 57

Odysseus, 9, 46, 47, 141, 188, 196
Okeanos, 15, 69
Olympia, 9, 25, *126*, 137, *166*, *192*
Orestes, 25, 141
Orpheus, 12, 28, 116
Orphic Hymns, 10, 116, 170
Orphic religion, 28, 116
Otto, Walter, quoted, 9, 54, 55, 70, 100, 105, 106, 107, 141, 205
Otus, 194
Ovid, 59, 72, 83, 85, 169

Paestum, *124*
Pan, 194, 195
Pandemus, 80
Pandora, 140, 175
Parthenon *see* Athens
Patmore, Coventry, 129
Patroclus, 26
Pegasus, 131
Peneus, 57–8
Pentheus, King, 106
Perera, S.B., quoted, 187, 188
Pericles, 142
Persephone (Kore), 15, 37, 78, 83, 178–83, *179*, 184, *185*
Perseus, 46, 141
Phaedra, 82
Phaethon, 131

Philostratus, quoted, 97
Phobos, 172
Pindar, quoted, 14, 15, 16, 81, 138
Pirithous, 27, 137
Plato, 13, 25, 26, 28, 57, 168, 196, 197
  Apology of Socrates, 7
  Cratylus, 147
  Epinomis, 26, 31
  Ion, 105
  Laws, 55, 100, 104
  Phaedrus, 60, 85, 169
  Republic, 27, 28, 31
  Statesman, 140
  Symposium, 13, 80
Plutarch, 55
Pluto *see* Hades
Polydeuces, 131
Polyhymnia, 57
Poseidon (Neptune), 14, 27, 31, 41, 42–7, *43*, *44–5*, *48*, 145, 161, 177
Powys, J.C., quoted, 60
Priapus, 172
Prometheus, 116, 131
Protagoras, 28
Proteus, 47
Psyche, 78, 80
Pygmalion, 83, 85
Pythia, 55

Rhea, 168
Rilke, Rainer Maria, quoted, 4, 30, 44, 120
Rumi, Jelaluddin, quoted, 104
Russell, George William, quoted, 203

Samothrace, *49*, *180*
Sarpedon, 26
Sarton, May, quoted, 75, 145
Schaffer, Peter, quoted, 42
Semele, 99, 100, 129
Shakespeare, W., quoted, 25, 29, 53, 72, 83, 161
Shelley, P.B., quoted, 53, 72
Sibyl, 59
Side (Turkey), *113*
Sikelianos, Angelos, quoted, 88, 120, 185
Silenus, *105*
Simon, Bennett, quoted, 106
Simonides, 28
Sipiora, Michael P., quoted, 78
Socrates, 28, 80, 81, 85, 187
Solzhenitsyn, Alexander, 85
Sophocles, 12, 15, 100
Sounion, *159*, *202*
Spretnak, Charlene, quoted, 183
Stechichorus, quoted, 129
Stoics, 120
Stratos, *134*
Swinburne, A., quoted, 53

Tarnus, Richard T., quoted, 32
Tartarus, 116
Tennyson, Alfred Lord, quoted, 131, 178, 180, 183

Terpsichore, 55
Thales, quoted, 8
Thalia, 55
Thasos, *195*
Thebes, 109, 129
Themis, 25, 116
Theseus, 27, 82, 108
Thomas, Gail, quoted, 185
Tiresias, 99, 161
Titans, 115, 116
Triptolemos, *179*
Triton, *51*
Troy, Trojan War, 42, 46, 47, 59, 129, 170, 172
Typhon, 129, 162, *167*

Underworld, 14, 15, 78, 83, 141, 178, 183, 187, 188, 194, 196, 197
Urania, 55
Uranus, 80

Venus *see* Aphrodite
Vesta *see* Hestia
Virgil, *Aeneid*, 10, 12, 187
Vulcan *see* Hephaistos
Vycinas, V., quoted, 54–5

Whitman, Walt, quoted, 205
Wilde, Oscar, quoted, 72
Wittgenstein, Ludwig, 31
Wordsworth, W., quoted, 152

Xenophon, 131

Yeats, W.B., quoted, 120

Zeus (Jupiter), 8, 9, 14, 15, 16, 25, 26, 27, 31, 32, *40*, 55, 60, 69, 80, 83, *92*, 100, 107, *114*, 115–31, *131*, *132*, 134, 137, 140, 142, 161, 162, 164, 168, 170, 172, 175, 176, 181, 183, 190, 194

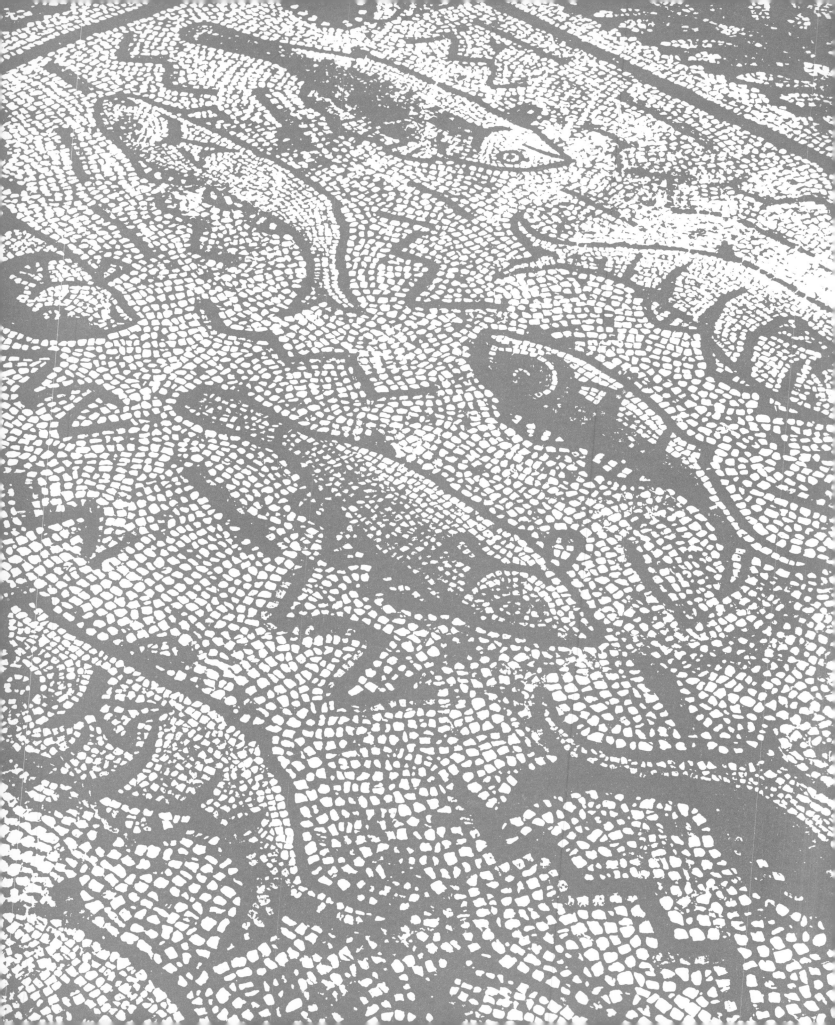